HUMAN CAPITAL IN
SOUTHERN DEVELOPMENT

1939-1963

HUMAN CAPITAL IN SOUTHERN DEVELOPMENT 1939-1963

Marshall R. Colberg

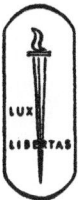

THE UNIVERSITY OF NORTH CAROLINA PRESS
CHAPEL HILL

Printed by The Seeman Printery, Durham, N. C.

PREFACE

THIS STUDY was made possible by a generous grant from the Inter-University Committee for Economic Research on the South. The grant provided an eleven-month leave of absence from other duties at Florida State University as well as funds for assistance in handling the voluminous statistical work involved. The writer is grateful indeed to the Inter-University Committee consisting of James M. Buchanan, Alan Cartter, Frank de Vyver, Melvin L. Greenhut, Maurice Lee, John McFerrin, James McKie, William H. Nicholls, B. U. Ratchford, Howard Schaller, Ernst Swanson, and W. Tate Whitman. Gratitude extends also to the Ford Foundation which provided the Committee funds for encouraging economic research on the South.

Several graduate students at Florida State University assisted the writer in the often tedious statistical compilations and calculations. James Clark and Douglas Windham performed outstandingly over long periods in this work. Patricia Moore and James Baker programmed some of the data for the electronic computer.

Numerous academicians contributed valuable counsel at various times. Milton Friedman first suggested to me about a decade ago that human capital was a potentially fertile field for research. His prediction has been well confirmed by the work of other economists. J. M. Buchanan and Ernst

Swanson made useful suggestions at an early stage in the work. My colleagues George Macesich, Melvin Greenhut, W. P. Dillingham, and Zarko Bilbija have shown consistent interest in the project and have contributed ideas at various points. Professor S. J. Knezevich read the chapter dealing with teachers' salaries and gave valuable advice in this connection. Several librarians, especially Miss Jo Kennedy, patiently sought out from their hiding places many seldom-used census reports and other documents.

A versatile and faithful secretarial staff consisting of Mrs. G. W. Jordan and Mrs. F. B. Kessler not only typed the manuscript but drew some preliminary charts and prepared the index. Finally, careful editing by The University of North Carolina Press has overcome many of the shortcomings which would otherwise have escaped the writer.

MARSHALL R. COLBERG

Tallahassee, Florida
May, 1965

CONTENTS

FIGURES

TABLES

HUMAN CAPITAL IN SOUTHERN DEVELOPMENT

1939-1963

*The great American problem of poverty and un-
derprivilege concerns Southern Labor.*

—Henry Simons[1]

CHAPTER I

THE SOUTH'S ECONOMIC PROBLEM

EVERY SOCIETY has an "economic problem" arising
from a limitation of its resources in the face of the insatiable
demands of its human inhabitants. At any point in history,
however, great differences exist between regions, broadly
or narrowly defined, in the extent to which the wants of
residents, on the average, are satisfied. In recent years
these differences have attracted increasing attention, especially because aid in developing the relatively backward
areas of the world has been deemed to be of great importance in the rivalry between world powers employing
dissimilar economic systems.

Increased preoccupation with problems of underde-
velopment of foreign nations has heightened interest in
uneven economic development within the United States.
The South is generally considered to be lagging behind
the rest of the country, although clearly many parts of the

1. "Some Reflections on Syndicalism," *Economic Policy for a Free
Society* (Chicago: University of Chicago Press, 1948), p. 135.

region are doing better economically than many parts of the non-South. Disparities in development have recently been emphasized by a national "distressed areas" program under which many parts of the country are considered to be in special need of federal loans, grants, and public works because of persistent unemployment and/or low average income.[2]

The present study reflects the current interest in analysis of uneven economic development within the United States. The approach differs, however, from other recent studies of regional development in that main emphasis is placed on "human capital" as a factor in southern economic development and on the movement and racial composition of this type of capital. Emphasis is placed on the relatively well educated portion of the population, and especially on professional persons, rather than on displaced farm workers and other impecunious groups. Other studies, published or under way, pay particular attention to the highly disadvantaged population.

DEFINING THE SOUTH

Anyone working on regional analysis soon encounters the problem of defining geographic areas in the most useful way. A book dealing with "the South," for example, will always include such typical states as Mississippi, Alabama, Georgia, and the Carolinas, but it is less clear whether Texas, Oklahoma, West Virginia, Delaware, Maryland and the District of Columbia should be included. In their well-known book on the region, Hoover and Ratchford include thirteen states: Alabama, Arkansas, Florida, Georgia, Kentucky, Louisiana, Mississippi, North Carolina, Oklahoma, South Carolina, Tennessee, Texas, and Virginia.[3] An important consideration in their selection was that "each of

2. Cf. Colberg, "Area Redevelopment and Related Federal Programs: Effects on the South," in M. L. Greenhut and T. Whitman, eds., *Essays in Southern Economic Development* (Chapel Hill: University of North Carolina Press, 1964); and Sar Levitan, *Federal Aid to Depressed Areas* (Baltimore: Johns Hopkins Press, 1964).

3. C. B. Hoover and B. C. Ratchford, *Economic Resources and Policies for the South* (New York: Macmillan, 1951), p. 1.

them is vitally concerned with the production of one or both of the two great staple cash crops of the region—cotton and tobacco." Nevertheless, Hoover and Ratchford noted that their analysis would be more pertinent to the Southeast than to Oklahoma and Texas.

Quite commonly, West Virginia is added to the thirteen states mentioned.[4] The importance of Bureau of the Census data, especially as related to population and manufacturing, is quite persuasive in causing the analyst also to add Maryland, Delaware, and the District of Columbia to the area designated as the South. Otherwise important data available only for such areas as the South Atlantic, East South Central, and West South Central states cannot be added to secure a total for the South. For the most part, the present book will use, on the pragmatic basis of better availability of data, the Bureau of the Census definition of the region. One objection to this definition of the South derives from untypical effects of the federal government in the District of Columbia and Maryland. However, these effects are also great in Virginia, which cannot well be excluded from the region.[5]

Where important social forces, such as segregation in schooling, can better be analyzed by means of a different definition of the South, the writer will not hesitate to depart, with a warning to the reader, from the Bureau of the Census classification. This *ad hoc* treatment of areas is in line with the Marshallian tradition of avoiding rigid definitions in economic analysis. It is consistent with the tendency of the "Chicago school" of economics to utilize relatively simple economic theorizing combined with definitions of variables ("money," for example) which may vary according to the problem under investigation. An opposite prac-

4. However, Edgar S. Dunn, Jr., has pointed out that in many respects West Virginia has a closer economic kinship to Pennsylvania and New England. See Dunn, *Recent Southern Economic Development*, University of Florida Monographs, Social Sciences, No. 14, Spring 1962 (Gainesville: University of Florida Press).

5. Problems in defining areas and analyzing areal data are carefully examined by O. D. Duncan, R. P. Cuzzort, and B. Duncan, *Statistical Geography* (Glencoe: The Free Press, 1961). See also D. J. Bogue and C. L. Beale, *Economic Areas of the United States* (Glencoe: The Free Press, 1961).

tice, followed by many economists, is to employ tighter definitions of economic variables in connection with a more complex array of theories to fit various circumstances. The willingness to define variables in an *ad hoc* fashion seems to be a good substitute for having on hand a wider range of theories to be applied *ad hoc* to particular problems.[6]

The need to have some flexibility in defining regions is well justified in a recent and ambitious volume by Perloff, Dunn, Lampard, and Muth.[7] They point out that the analyst's problem differs from that of the statistician who must of necessity present data in consistent, general-purpose classifications. Although they present a regional grouping of states early in the book, these authors state that they "employ the grouping...merely as a point of departure and feel free to change the designation wherever this seems appropriate." Similar license will be taken in the present study but deviations in the regional definition should be easier to keep in mind since attention will be focused on only one region—the South.

In concentrating on the South, however, it is important also to present comparable data pertaining to the United States as a whole, or better, to the "non-South." To examine a region without reference to the rest of the country is comparable to engaging in partial equilibrium analysis of an industry without considering inevitable general equilibrium effects. Milton Friedman has led a methodological advance, pointing out, for example, that a demand curve constructed in the ordinary way (money income and all other prices constant) is illogical. Any consideration of a lower price for a given commodity, with a consequent increase in amount demanded, incorrectly implies that the community can consume more of this good without reducing its con-

6. In his essay "The Chicago School" in *Towards a More General Theory of Value* (New York: Oxford University Press, 1957), Edward H. Chamberlin claims that Stigler, Friedman, and other critics of "monopolistic competition" also live in "*ad hoc* houses" (p. 305). The distinction between *ad hoc* definition of variables and *ad hoc* selection of a pertinent theory is not made, however.

7. H. S. Perloff, E. S. Dunn, Jr., E. E. Lampard, and R. F. Muth, *Regions, Resources, and Economic Growth* (Baltimore: Johns Hopkins Press, 1960), p. 7.

sumption of other goods.[8] The ordinary (Hicksian) demand curve is, consequently, inconsistent with the basic accompanying assumptions of fixity in the quantity of available resources and full employment.

Important applications of this methodological view have been made in the field of public finance. It can be misleading, for example, in examining the effects of a new tax to consider only the collection side, since government expenditures and/or cash balances are certain to be affected also. Similarly, in analyzing the effects of interest payments to foreign creditors, it must be kept in mind that domestic productivity has been enhanced by prior receipt of capital from abroad.[9]

If labor leaves the South, for example, it necessarily enters the non-South. The region's per capita income is affected by a change in its labor-capital ratio, and a change in this ratio also occurs in the non-South. Neglect of the latter change would tend to cause an understatement of the effect of the migration in bringing per capita income in the South closer to that of the non-South. Similarly, the acquisition of a new plant by one community is likely to deprive another community of a similar plant—at least in an "opportunity cost" sense. Realization of this relationship can affect one's appraisal of government policies designed to alter the location of new plants. (Publicity regarding the plant is certain to stress the benefit side and to neglect the cost side.)

One important difference between analysis and propaganda lies in the care with which essential elements of the *whole* picture are shown. A community which is attempt-

8. Milton Friedman, "The Marshallian Demand Curve," *Essays in Positive Economics* (Chicago: The University of Chicago Press, 1953), p. 62.

9. Cf. James M. Buchanan, *Public Principles of Public Debt* (Homewood, Ill.: Richard D. Irwin, Inc., 1958), chap. II. This chapter contains an excellent summary discussion of methodology in connection with public finance. See also J. M. Buchanan, *Fiscal Theory and Political Economy* (Chapel Hill: University of North Carolina Press, 1960), especially essays VI and VII. For an application of a similar methodological viewpoint to the problem of inflation see George Macesich, "Current Inflation Theory: Considerations on Methodology," *Social Research*, Autumn, 1961, pp. 321-30.

ing to attract new industry may stress its low property taxes but is certain not to point out a consequent deficiency in the public services that are provided. Economic theorizing that incorporates important general equilibrium considerations avoids being unnecessarily partial (in both senses of the word).

STATISTICS OF SOUTHERN DEVELOPMENT

It is useful to present at the outset some summary data pertaining to the recent economic development of the South. The amount of such information that could be compiled is almost limitless, of course. Consequently, only data that are considered most basically informative will be shown here. For more detailed information, the original sources may be consulted.

Probably the most useful single measure of relative economic development within a country is per capita income, since this pertains most closely to want-satisfaction on the average. As shown in Table 1-1, per capita personal income in the South is well below that of the nation as a whole. During the years of World War II the difference decreased substantially in percentage, but not in absolute terms, and a modest further closing of the gap occurred between 1950 and 1960. The ratio of southern to national per capita personal income in 1960 was 78.6 per cent.

Improvement in the ratio has come from two sources: a relative increase in personal income and a relative decrease in population. Of the two, the increase in income has had the greater influence. The South, nevertheless, remains a low income region by national standards. Per capita personal income in 1960 was substantially lower than in any of the other major regions of the United States. In absolute real income per capita, the South's deficiency was about the same in 1962 as in 1929.[10]

The South is a relatively homogeneous region from the viewpoint of 1960 per capita income. Table 1-2 shows that all of the southern states, with the exception of Delaware,

10. E. J. R. Booth, "Interregional Income Differences," *Southern Economic Journal,* July, 1964, p. 50.

TABLE 1-1. THE SOUTH'S POPULATION AND INCOME: 1940-1960

Census and Region	Personal Income ($ million)	Population (million)	Per Capita Personal Income ($)
1940			
United States	78.5	132.2	594
South	16.4	41.7	394
South as % of U.S.	20.9%	31.5%	66.3%
1950			
United States	225.5	151.3	1491
South	53.3	47.2	1129
South as % of U.S.	23.6%	31.2%	75.7%
1960			
United States	400.0	179.3	2231
South	96.4	55.0	1753
South as % of U.S.	24.1%	30.7%	78.6%

Source: *U.S. Census of Population, 1960,* and U.S. Department of Commerce, *Statistical Abstract of the United States, 1962.*

Maryland, and the District of Columbia, were below the national average in this respect. It will be remembered that Delaware, Maryland, and the District of Columbia are being included in the regional definition more for statistical convenience than for similarity of most economic attributes. In most cases they have little effect on the data for the region as a whole. Among the other southern states, per capita income is highest in Florida and Texas and lowest in Mississippi and Arkansas.

To a considerable extent, the problem of low per capita income in the South is one of low income for non-white persons, especially those with rural residence. White men and women in the South had lower median incomes in 1959 than the comparable persons in other regions, but divergences are not so great as those indicated in Table 1-2, which covers non-whites as well. Table 1-3, taken from the 1960 population census, shows median incomes for urban, rural non-farm, and rural farm residents. Low earnings on southern farms are especially evident. In the case of

TABLE 1-2. PER CAPITA INCOME IN SOUTHERN STATES, 1962

State	Per Capita Personal Income 1962 (dollars)	Per cent of U.S.
United States	2366	100
Alabama	1567	66
Arkansas	1504	64
Delaware	3102	131
District of Columbia	3219	136
Florida	2044	86
Georgia	1759	74
Kentucky	1712	72
Louisiana	1705	72
Maryland	2683	113
Mississippi	1285	54
North Carolina	1732	73
Oklahoma	1905	81
South Carolina	1545	65
Texas	2013	85
Tennessee	1702	72
Virginia	2018	85
West Virginia	1810	76

Source: U.S. Department of Commerce, *Survey of Current Business,* August, 1963.

urban residents, the smaller size of southern cities probably explains some of the deficiency in median income compared with other regions. Lower educational attainment also accounts for some of the deficit.

Much has been written about the decline in farm employment in the United States. Among the causes are increased mechanization and other technological improvements, a generally low income elasticity of demand for agricultural products, greatly increased competition from synthetic fibers, and government price supports which diminish both exports and domestic consumption. Varying definitions and sources of data cause difficulty in measuring the influence of this decline on the nation and the South. However, according to an important source,[11] the total number

11. *Statistical Abstract of the United States, 1962,* and *1962 County and City Data Book,* U.S. Dept. of Commerce, Bureau of the Census.

TABLE 1-3.   MEDIAN INCOME OF PERSONS WITH INCOME, 1959
(dollars)

Region and Sex	Urban	White Rural Non-Farm	Rural Farm	Urban	Non-White Rural Non-Farm	Rural Farm
Males						
Northeast	4752	4205	2766	3310	2307	1817
North Central	5056	3937	2438	3488	1424	1042
South	4247	2862	1812	2153	1145	744
West	5096	3833	3247	3702	2104	2121
Females						
Northeast	1827	1280	961	1735	956	680
North Central	1525	964	831	1357	726	449
South	1504	963	794	831	468	358
West	1662	1031	823	1633	834	748

Source: *U.S. Census of Population: 1960. General Social and Economic Characteristics*, United States Summary, Table 139.

of employed persons in agriculture declined from about 9.5 million in 1940 to about 5.7 million in 1960. Agricultural employment in the South fell from about 4.2 million to about 1.7 million during the same period, accounting for almost two thirds of the national decline.

Manufacturing employment in the United States increased by about 6 million persons during the two decades. In the South the increase in this employment was almost 2 million. However, the gain in manufacturing employment in the region was not so great as the loss of jobs on the farms. Due to the South's gain in employment in wholesale and retail trade (almost 1.6 million), government, transportation, education and other activities, a net gain of about 5.6 million in employed persons occurred during the twenty-year period. Unfortunately, great numbers of displaced agricultural workers in the South have not been able to switch over to the expanding activities because of a lack of skills, lack of information, lack of intra-regional mobility, and a greater degree of racial discrimination in non-farm employment.[12] This has stimulated a great outmigration of low-income persons, especially non-whites, from the South.

An impression of the effect of this movement can be gained from Table 1-4. Despite a high birth rate, the non-white population in the South increased by only 1.5 million between the 1940 and 1960 censuses, compared with an 11.8 million increase of white people. Sharp absolute declines in the non-white population occurred in Arkansas, Mississippi, and West Virginia; a moderate decline took place in Oklahoma, and a slight decline occurred in Alabama. The white population declined in two states—Arkansas and West Virginia. For the South as a whole, the share of the nation's non-white population declined from 74 per cent in 1940 to 56 per cent in 1960.

TABLE 1-4.   RACIAL COMPOSITION OF SOUTHERN POPULATION:
1940-1960

Census Year	White Population		Non-White Population	
	No. (million)	Per cent of Southern Population	No. (million)	Per cent of Southern Population
1940	31.7	76.0	10.0	24.0
1950	36.8	77.9	10.4	22.1
1960	43.5	79.1	11.5	20.9

Source: *U.S. Census of Population,* 1940, 1950, 1960.

Americans continually move in large numbers into and out of every state and within each state. When net migration for an area, however broadly or narrowly defined, is large in magnitude, important social consequences ensue. These may also be generated by a radical change in the *composition* of population even in the absence of net migration. The economist is interested in population movements particularly as they affect such variables as income

12. In terms of the analysis presented by Gary S. Becker in *The Economics of Discrimination* (Chicago: University of Chicago Press, 1957), the smaller degree of discrimination against non-whites in agriculture may be traceable to the competitiveness of the field and to the lesser degree of personal association between employer and employee.

and its distribution, the value of land and other geographically fixed capital assets, wage rates, unemployment, productivity, the location of industry, and government control of the economy.

Some recent studies are especially useful in disclosing the nature of population movements with respect to the South for the inter-census period 1950-1960. It has been pointed out[13] that during this decade net migration from the South (defined as in the present study) was about 1.4 million persons, and that this was almost equal to the net outmigration of Negroes from the region. Movements of white people into and out of the region were roughly in balance. In terms of Table 1-4, the white population of the South would have remained at about the 1950 level of 36.8 million had it not been for the natural increase. Non-white population would have declined to 9.0 million in 1960 instead of increasing to 11.5 million. These figures reflect the substantially higher birth rate for non-whites.

It is well known that young people migrate in greater proportion to their numbers than do older people. This is due to a combination of their own search for better opportunities and the search of their parents for such opportunities. Taeuber points out that more than half of the teen-age non-whites residing in Mississippi in 1950 had moved out of the state by 1960.

Rural outmigration between 1950 and 1960 occurred in all states except Florida, Colorado, Connecticut, and Nevada, according to James M. Henderson.[14] For the forty-eight states of the conterminous United States he estimated a net movement of 10.5 million persons from farms and other rural areas to cities. The South's rural outmigration rate and its urban inmigration rate both substantially exceeded the corresponding national rates. Henderson shows that non-white urban migration rates are higher outside the

13. Conrad Taeuber, "Some Recent Population Trends in the South," a paper presented at the Conference on Area Development, Athens, Georgia, January 8, 1962.

14. "Some General Aspects of Regional Developments During the 1950-1960 Decade," a paper prepared for the Second Annual Conference, Inter-University Committee for Economic Research on the South, New Orleans, February 23-24, 1962.

South. He interestingly characterizes the District of Columbia, Illinois, Missouri, New York, and Pennsylvania as "mature-urban areas for whites, but frontier areas for non-whites."

While measures of net migration are highly informative, they can be misleading if they convey an impression of one-way traffic. Less information is collected on two-way movements, but available data show that even such states as West Virginia, Arkansas, and Mississippi have many inmigrants each year. This is illustrated in Table 1-5 which shows movements into and out of the southern states (and the District of Columbia) during one year prior to the 1950 census of population. The data are based on a sample of enumerated persons who were asked whether they lived in the same state one year earlier. Large net gains by such states as Texas, Florida, and Maryland were nevertheless accompanied by outmigration roughly two thirds as great in volume as inmigration. Inmigrants to Mississippi, Arkansas, and West Virginia were about four-fifths as numerous as outmigrants.

A partial explanation for the large number of persons moving into Mississippi may be found, according to an economist who has specialized in migration research, in the heterogeneity of occupations and industries.[15] Outmigrants may be unqualified for jobs in the expanding sectors within the state. Other inmigrants may be retiring there due to a relatively low cost-of-living or may be disillusioned outmigrants of previous years, according to Sjaastad.

One of the basic hypotheses being investigated in the present book is that "human capital" should be entering the South while "labor" should be leaving. This may account for a good deal of the two-way movement shown in Table 1-5. A bit of evidence pointing in this direction is contained in a population census report for 1950.[16] The number of male inmigrants to the South in one year prior to

15. Larry A. Sjaastad, "The Costs and Returns of Human Migration," *Journal of Political Economy*, Supplement (October, 1962), p. 81.

16. *U.S. Census of Population: 1950*. Vol. IV, *Special Reports*, Part 4, Chapter D, Population Mobility—Characteristics of Migrants, Table 11, p. 198 and Table 12, p. 270.

that census was 38.4 thousand of professional, technical, and managerial personnel plus non-farm proprietors. These men are largely college graduates. The number of out-migrants from the South in these occupations was 26.4 thousand. At the other end of the occupational ladder, farm laborers, foremen, and non-farm laborers combined left the South in greater numbers than they entered—about 26.4 thousand left while 21.6 thousand entered.

A more recent but less detailed view of two-way migration can be obtained from Table 1-6. The gains and losses from migration between 1955 and 1960 are shown for southern regions. Non-white persons had a net outmigration

TABLE 1-5. TWO-WAY MIGRATION IN ONE YEAR

State	Inmigrants	Outmigrants	Net Migration
Alabama	63,690	79,260	−15,570
Arkansas	67,540	85,060	−17,520
Delaware	9,775	10,275	− 500
District of Columbia	48,775	73,360	−24,585
Florida	186,025	119,675	+66,350
Georgia	94,305	93,905	+ 400
Kentucky	67,555	81,195	−13,640
Louisiana	66,710	62,575	+ 4,135
Maryland	98,190	66,115	+32,075
Mississippi	51,865	62,515	−10,650
North Carolina	85,030	83,485	+ 1,545
Oklahoma	99,540	95,725	+ 3,815
South Carolina	46,250	52,115	− 5,865
Texas	255,210	186,325	+68,885
Tennessee	103,100	90,945	+12,155
Virginia	134,525	112,505	+22,020
West Virginia	40,375	49,155	− 8,780

Source: *U.S. Census of Population: 1950.* Vol. IV, *Special Reports,* Part 4, Chapter B, Population Mobility—States and State Economic Areas, Table 8, p. 32.

from all three subregions but white people moved into the South Atlantic region in large numbers. This caused a net loss in white people in the East South Central and West

South Central regions. It can be inferred from Table 1-6 that for the South Atlantic region much of this net inmigration can be accounted for by the movement of people into Florida. Since many new residents of this state are retired persons, their inmigration is not traceable to a search for better economic opportunity—in the usual meaning of the term, at least.

TABLE 1-6. GAINS AND LOSSES FROM MIGRATION, 1955 TO 1960

Race and Subregion	Inmigrants	Outmigrants	Net Migration
White			
South Atlantic	1,697,365	1,133,980	+563,385
East South Central	577,815	765,919	−188,104
West South Central	817,525	918,617	−101,092
Non-White			
South Atlantic	93,324	189,347	− 96,023
East South Central	44,466	159,519	−115,053
West South Central	54,811	114,307	− 59,496

Source: *U.S. Census of Population: 1960. Subject Reports. Lifetime and Recent Migration,* Final Report PC(2)-2D, Table 4, p. 16.

LABOR AND HUMAN CAPITAL

While considerable southern progress is revealed in the statistical information just presented, it is clear that the region is still a relatively underdeveloped one. The basic remedy lies in a continued and augmented flow of material and human capital into the South and an outmigration of labor possessing low marginal-value productivity. Movement by individuals out of the low-productivity category by means of appropriate education is also promising. Further, a movement of persons *within* the region can aid development if the moves result in better economic opportunities. The best opportunity in this direction usually lies in the migration of low-productivity farm workers into southern cities. As already indicated, urban inmigration in the South has been based quite heavily on rural outmigration within the region itself.

Although outmigration of low-income families is a direct way of raising per capita income in a region, it is probably a less satisfactory means than the inmigration of capital. John Moes has argued persuasively that it is desirable to strive for the creation of economic conditions under which people will have a free choice between migrating or remaining at home and working at a lower rate of pay.[17] Moes advocates local subsidies to industry as a means of securing enough industry to permit a choice between alternatives that are not unreasonably far apart. The adverse effects of outmigration on the value of immobile property, on retail sales, and on opportunities for local professional persons are also important reasons for preferring that jobs move to people rather than that people move to jobs. Some "multiplier" effect on local income can be expected to occur when new industry is established. That is, community income will expand by somewhat more than the amount of new wage and salary payments to residents.[18] Similarly, negative multiplier effects are associated with outmigration.

The common idea that outmigration of labor from the South is desirable needs to be examined more closely. As will be discussed in some detail in Chapter 2, there has recently been much emphasis on "human capital," that is, investment in individuals, primarily by means of formal education. If human capital is treated as a factor of production separate from labor, it is apparent that an inmigration of well-trained individuals is preferable to an outmigration. Such persons not only earn above-average incomes but are also highly important in raising the productivity of material capital and of ordinary labor.

A basic objective of the present study will be to divide the contribution of the human agent into the services of "labor" and those of "human capital" for the southern region. It is believed that this division will provide useful insights into important aspects of regional development.

17. *Local Subsidies for Industry* (Chapel Hill: University of North Carolina Press, 1962).

18. Some measurements of local multipliers due to inmigration are given by Charles Tiebout, "Community Income Multipliers: A Population Growth Model," *Journal of Regional Science*, II (Spring, 1960).

For example, is human capital moving into or out of the region, thus assisting or impeding the region's development? What are the effects of racial segregation on the inter-regional movements of human capital and labor? Is the South attracting "labor intensive" manufacturing, or can its new industry better be characterized as "human capital intensive?" What are some of the demonstrated and anticipated effects of federal judicial and legislative actions on southern development? What are some salient differences between southern states in relation to the above questions?

Attention will be concentrated almost entirely on the period since 1939. Those who are interested in the historical sweep of southern economic development can find a great deal of interesting material elsewhere.[19] Concentration on the recent development of the region will permit more intensive use of statistical materials (especially the population censuses of 1940, 1950, and 1960) than would be possible if a wider time span were used. Also, the period since 1939 is of special interest because it includes World War II, because it comprehends a time of great renascence of interest in education, because it involves a tremendous increase in the scope and size of the federal government, and because it is a period in which legal and other institutions affecting racial relations have undergone great change.

While the present study will contain a good deal of statistical information pertaining to the South since 1939, an attempt will be made not to present data for their own sake but rather to use them to test hypotheses which are

19. Some useful and relatively recent works in addition to those already cited are: William H. Nicholls, *Southern Tradition and Regional Progress* (Chapel Hill: University of North Carolina Press, 1960); Thomas D. Clark, *The Emerging South* (New York: Oxford University Press, 1961); Howard W. Odum and Harry E. Moore, *American Regionalism* (New York: Henry Holt & Co., 1938); Rupert B. Vance, *All These People: The Nation's Human Resources in the South* (Chapel Hill: University of North Carolina Press, 1945).

An excellent bibliography, as well as an interesting summary of writings on southern development, is given by Clarence H. Danhof in "Three Decades of Thought on the South's Economic Problem," a paper prepared for the Second Annual Conference of the Inter-University Committee for Economic Research on the South, New Orleans, February 23-24, 1962.

relevant to economic development.[20] Nevertheless, the writer hopes and believes that some of the statistical series will be useful to other investigators, especially those interested in research on "human capital."

20. Recent information on such matters as southern income, population, employment, and value added by manufacture may be found in Greenhut and Whitman (eds.), *Essays in Southern Economic Development.*

The difference between the most dissimilar characters, between a philosopher and a common street porter, seems to arise not so much from nature, as from habit, custom, and education.
— Adam Smith, *Wealth of Nations*

CHAPTER II
HUMAN CAPITAL AS AN
ECONOMIC RESOURCE

AS IS SO OFTEN THE CASE, ideas of current interest to economists were at least touched upon by Adam Smith in his great book, *The Wealth of Nations.* His strong tendency to place environment above heredity led him to make excellent observations regarding investment in the individual. The following statement is remarkably clear on this point:

> A man educated at the expence of much labour and time to any of those employments which require extraordinary dexterity and skill, may be compared to one of those expensive machines. The work which he learns to perform, it must be expected, over and above the usual wages of common labour, will replace to him the whole expence of his education, with at least the ordinary profits of an equally valuable capital. It must do this in a reasonable time, regard being had to the very uncertain duration of human life, in the same manner as to the more certain duration of the machine.[1]

1. Adam Smith, *The Wealth of Nations* (Modern Library edition, 1937), p. 101.

Smith and the other early classical economists used the term profits to include both interest and profit, as the terms are currently used. Capital was usually considered to be a fund out of which wages and other costs were met, and in agriculture, at least, the fund was considered to be periodically advanced and recouped by its owner. The above quotation can consequently be interpreted to mean that investment in education will ordinarily bring the individual at least an average interest return on this cost over and above replacement of the entire sum expended on education. Under favorable circumstances, such as a persistent increase in the relevant demand, or unusual longevity, the return to the individual may be much greater, while under adverse circumstances it may be much lower. The quotation comes from Smith's famous discussion of the causes of differences in pecuniary compensation in various occupations. Since it is part of his treatment of differences that arise from the "difficulty and expence of learning the business," it does not pertain directly to the "value of an individual" or to the aggregate value of "human capital."[2]

Many other economists since Smith (and probably before) have made somewhat similar statements regarding investment in the individual. Nassau Senior (in 1836) used the term "immaterial" capital to denote the abilities built up in the individual through education. He observed that the use of immaterial capital necessarily involves labor on the part of the owner and that his income is consequently a mixture of wages and interest.[3] Irving Fisher put it this way: "When a young man studies law, medicine, journalism, music, or prepares for any other profession, he is investing in his own person, with the hope that sums thus invested

2. Louis I. Dublin and Alfred J. Lotka, in *The Money Value of a Man* (New York: Ronald Press, 1946), make extensive calculations of the value of a man from an insurance point of view, emphasizing the loss to a family if the head of the family dies. They point out that the first such calculations were presented by Sir William Petty in *Political Arithmetick* (1699).

3. Cf. M. R. Colberg, "The Value and Distribution Theory of Nassau William Senior," unpublished master's thesis, University of Chicago, 1938, p. 39.

may ultimately be returned to him (with interest). The same is true of physical training."[4]

Alfred Marshall observed that the return on the skill of a miner may be regarded as quasi-rent much as the return on a machine is so regarded, and that a deduction must be made for wear and tear when the special return on his skill is being estimated.[5]

Marshall also considered the related problem of what to call the extra income earned by extraordinary natural abilities (p. 577). He considered such income to be a combination of components resulting from chance, opportunity, start in life, return on capital invested in special training, exceptionally hard work, or the possession of rare natural gifts. While Marshall did not attempt to show how to separate the individual contributions of these components, his observation constitutes something of a warning against considering all of the extra income of educated persons to be a return on investment in education. On the average, education is correlated positively with the other factors that Marshall names.

Edwin Cannan commented interestingly on Marshall's concept of quasi-rent on personal qualities.[6] He pointed out that an important difference between property and human qualities is that the former can earn income for its owner while the owner "goes off to golf," whereas personal qualities can only be used by the person in whom they are vested. The conclusion Cannan reaches is that "the traditional classification in which the income derived from labour is treated as a whole—is to be preferred to the entirely fanciful classification of labour incomes into income from pure labour and income from the labourers' property in their natural and acquired talents" (p. 329).

Cannan is undoubtedly right that separation of the labor and capital components of wages and salaries is difficult and must be somewhat arbitrary. However, he does not seem

4. *The Nature of Capital and Income* (New York: Macmillan, 1912), p. 170.

5. *Principles of Economics* (8th ed.; London: Macmillan, 1930), p. 576.

6. *A Review of Economic Theory* (London: P. S. King and Son, Ltd., 1929), p. 327.

to realize that classification of economic variables need not be rigid but should be *ad hoc*, that is, designed to meet the needs of whatever problem is at hand. If the problem is related to the proper amount of life insurance for the head of a family to carry—the main problem analyzed by Dublin and Lotka—it is not necessary to separate the average income earned at any particular age in any occupation into labor and immaterial capital components. The loss to the family in case of the death of the main breadwinner does not depend on this separation. On the other hand if the problem is to estimate the gain in income due to education, or to estimate how much an individual or society should invest in education, a separation of labor and human capital incomes is necessary.

In order to estimate the capitalized value of a wage or salary earner for life insurance purposes it is appropriate to deduct from his anticipated yearly earnings the amount he will spend on himself. This amount will not be available to the rest of the family if he lives and, presumably, need not be consumed by beneficiaries in the event of his death.[7]

If the problem is to evaluate the human capital of a region, it appears to be more appropriate to deduct from the anticipated lifetime earnings of a college graduate, for example, the earnings that he would probably have had without education beyond grammar school. This is in line with the remarks made by Smith, Senior, Marshall, and the other classical and neo-classical economists already mentioned. The procedure raises the question "When does education cease to be primarily consumption and begin to be primarily investment in future earning power?" The answer must be arbitrary in any statistical estimates. In the United States it seems reasonable to consider education at the grade school level to be necessary for securing any substantial employment, and to consider subsequent education as the means of building immaterial capital into the individual.

T. W. Schultz assumes in a recent essay that families

7. Anticipation of the added consumption possible due to relief from further life insurance premiums in the event of death of the principal breadwinner should enter into the calculation, the effect being to reduce the amount of insurance needed.

and students do not think of elementary education as investment, that they look upon high school as both consumption and investment, and consider college or university education mainly or wholly as investment.[8]   Professor Schultz also points out however that the return to elementary education is very large, so he does not choose to consider investment in the individual to take place only beyond the eighth grade.   For purposes of measuring the return to investment in education, the costs and returns from elementary education should undoubtedly be included. In assessing the regional allocation of human capital it appears preferable to consider elementary education a component of labor, and high school and subsequent education a component of human capital.   Otherwise there is no room for labor as a factor of production.   Since the types of employment for which high school, and especially college and university education, qualify the recipient are usually so different from the types available to those with elementary education only, it appears useful for purposes of the present study to follow the approach indicated.   *Ad hoc* definition of variables has merit so long as the reader realizes that definitions may vary from writer to writer.

Recent writers have emphasized that there are numerous ways to build human capital in addition to investing in formal education.   Gary Becker has summarized these in "on-the-job training, medical care, vitamin consumption, and acquiring information about the economic system."[9] Larry Sjaastad has analyzed migration as an investment in the human agent.[10]   Also, experience on a job, especially if it involves complex skills, is clearly a way of building human capital even in the absence of further formal schooling or on-the-job training.   This build-up provides a basic justifica-

8. "Education and Economic Growth," *Social Forces Influencing American Education* (Chicago: University of Chicago Press, 1961), p. 75.

9. Gary S. Becker, "Investment in Human Capital: a Theoretical Analysis," *Journal of Political Economy, Supplement* (October 1962), p. 9.

10. *Ibid.*, pp. 80-93.   Also see articles in this supplement devoted to investment in human beings by T. W. Schultz, J. Mincer, G. Stigler, B. Weisbrod, E. Denison, and S. Mushkin.   An extensive bibliography on costs and returns to education is given by T. W. Schultz in a recent book, *The Economic Value of Education* (New York and London: Columbia University Press, 1963).

tion for periodic salary increases for such groups as university professors. Nevertheless, the importance of formal education is so great that interesting work can be done by considering the relation of earnings to such education alone.

ABSTINENCE AS A FACTOR IN HUMAN CAPITAL

The notion of "abstinence" on the part of the capitalist was suggested by Smith, Ricardo, Nebenius, Scrope and others but was developed and utilized most fully by Senior.[11] These writers were not careful to distinguish between abstinence as merely the *conduct* of saving or maintaining a stock of capital and the *painfulness* of this conduct connoted by the term. This led to attacks by socialist writers who pointed out the unreality of mental pain connected with receiving interest on large estates, especially when they were inherited.

In its application to human rather than material capital, the Socialist criticism is less appropriate. In order to acquire an education that will significantly build up his earning power, an individual must abstain from other, usually more pleasant, uses of his time in order to study. In addition, he must abstain from consuming the goods and services which he might have purchased with funds spent on such items as tuition and textbooks. And more important, he must abstain from the purchase of goods which could have been acquired with earnings foregone during the period of his education.

If he is to earn interest income on material capital which he owns, the capitalist must continue to abstain from selling these assets and devoting the proceeds to more immediate consumption. This conduct may be rather painful to the minor capitalist but scarcely to a millionaire. The same possibility of speedily liquidating a stock of human capital and consuming the proceeds does not exist. However, abstinence is still required if human capital is to earn interest in the sense that the owner must refrain from spending his time on inferior work, long vacations, or early retirement. Ownership of a large stock of material capital can provide

11. Colberg, *op. cit.*, p. 11.

both the inducement and the means for failing to use human capital.[12]

HUMAN CAPITAL AS AN ACCUMULATING STOCK

It has been emphasized by Professor Frank H. Knight, that in societies about which we have any reason to theorize, capital is properly considered to be an accumulating stock of heterogeneous goods capable of yielding income, viewed as a value magnitude, with specific items continually depreciating and being replaced.[13] The same concept is applicable to "human capital" although in a non-slave economy the individual cannot be bought and sold outright.

The existing stock of material capital represents an accumulation from the beginning of time, in Knight's view, since capital goods as well as labor, enter into the production of further capital goods. As new capital goods are produced they embody the technological knowledge available at the time, with economic factors playing a part in determining the form of additions to the stock as well as in the maintenance of old items.

Quite similarly, the present stock of human capital represents an accumulation from the beginning of time. Available knowledge and technology, together with economic factors, enter into the creation of new "human capital goods" and also help determine the value of existing immaterial capital. In general, an economic system, whether it is organized on a free market or on an authoritarian basis, should be more successful in keeping its human capital in the right geographic locations than in keeping material capital well allocated geographically. Many capital goods (buildings, bridges, irrigation ditches, roads, growing trees)

12. A steeply progressive tax on money income is especially effective in causing human capital to be unutilized or under-utilized. An individual who has a great deal of income from material capital may not find it worthwhile to use his talents to earn additional income taxable at high marginal rates if he finds such work to be more onerous than leisure or untaxed "do it yourself" projects.

13. See, for example, F. H. Knight, "The Quantity of Capital and the Rate of Interest," *Journal of Political Economy*, XLIV (August, 1936), 437.

cannot be moved at all once they are in place. There is, of course, often a reluctance on the part of educated people —as well as others—to move in response to economic incentives, but in general it appears that within a given country, at least, the obstacles to movement of human capital goods are inherently less formidable than for most material capital goods.[14]

Geographic mobility of material capital occurs mainly via *new* capital goods, funds for which are obtained from personal and business savings and taxation. To a degree this is true also of human capital, since young people are more mobile geographically than their elders. However, there appears to be much greater inter-regional mobility among older individuals who embody much immaterial capital than for used material capital goods.

Funds invested in fixed capital equipment in one region can usually be moved from one place to another only gradually through under-maintenance and under-replacement. Assets thus accumulated in a liquid form may be invested elsewhere, but in many cases substantial under-maintenance is not feasible. A retail store, for example, must be kept in fairly good repair as long as it is used for this purpose because of the loss of customers that would result from a shoddy appearance. As a consequence, depreciation reserves seem to be less important than savings (both voluntary and "forced" by taxation or inflation) as a source of regional mobility of the stock of material capital. To a degree, nevertheless, it is possible to move the funds invested in material capital goods without moving the goods themselves.

The same possibility is open in the case of human capital. An educated individual can skimp on the maintenance of his immaterial capital in order to invest more heavily in the education of his children, who may then choose to reside elsewhere. While a movement of persons occurs when the children migrate, there is in this case also some attrition in

14. Some capital goods devoted to transportation, such as airplanes, trucks, boxcars, taxicabs, and ships are by nature easy to transfer geographically. The same is true of many of the smaller capital goods such as typewriters.

the capital invested in the parent who remains behind. The same sort of capital movement can occur if heavy teaching loads permit the professor little time for research. His human capital then tends to be under-maintained and the resulting funds are invested in students, many of whom will not remain in the region. This sort of capital movement appears to be a real problem in parts of the South, but this is not to imply that the problem does not also arise elsewhere. The difficulty in measuring this sort of movement of human capital tends to prevent remedial measures. In contrast, the outright relocation of a manufacturing plant arouses strong emotions.

Indirect evidence that human capital is quite mobile geographically is found in wage and salary data published by the federal government. It is well known that wage differentials between the South and the non-South are greatest for the least skilled workers. The recently expanded annual survey of occupational wage rates by the Bureau of Labor Statistics shows median wage rates in the South for unskilled plant labor to be 67 to 79 per cent of the national median. Skilled maintenance personnel in the South were paid at wage rates ranging from 83 to 94 per cent of the national median.[15] It seems probable that this situation is due mainly to greater inter-regional mobility as the level of skill rises.

Friedman and Kuznets found regional differences in incomes from independent professional practice to be small compared with those due to community size.[16] The latter differences would seem to be due mainly to non-pecuniary attributes of communities of different sizes and to systematic quality differences of professional persons rather than to unwillingness to change locations within the same region.

Support for the idea that inter-regional mobility of the more educated population is substantial is also found in the 1950 census. Median income for white males with 16 or

15. Toivo P. Kanninen, "Wage Differences Among Labor Markets," *Monthly Labor Review*, LXXXV (June, 1962), 619.

16. Milton Friedman and Simon Kuznets, *Income from Independent Professional Practice* (New York: National Bureau of Economic Research, 1945), p. 197.

more years of education was actually higher in the South than in the non-South from age 20 through 34. At higher ages salaries in the South were somewhat lower. Highest earnings came in the 45 to 54 age bracket, the median being $5520 per year in the South and $5637 in the non-South.[17] A study by Morton Zeman of census data for 1940 shows a similar tendency. In the 22 to 24 year age bracket, white urban males with 16 or more years of education had a mean wage or salary of $1062 per year in the South and $1014 in the non-South. In the 25 to 29 age bracket, Southern incomes led slightly, $1666 to $1660.[18]

While none of the data cited may be said to apply strictly to "human capital," they strongly suggest that there is sufficient mobility of such capital to prevent areas of important "surplus" or "deficit" of this factor of production. Instead, the stock of human capital seems to be at all times fairly well adjusted to regional supplies of labor and material capital. If this is true, movements in human capital should depend not on relative stocks of these other factors but on *changes* in these stocks. This hypothesis will be elaborated in the next chapter.

17. Data are from the 1950 Census of Population as presented by W. Hochwald and M. Megee, "The Industrial Composition of the South and Its Bearing upon the Economic Development of the Region," a paper prepared for the Second Annual Conference of the Inter-University Committee for Economic Research on the South, New Orleans, February 23-24, 1962.

18. Morton Zeman, "A Quantitative Analysis of White—Non-White Income Differentials in the United States," unpublished Ph.D. Dissertation, University of Chicago, 1955, p. 81.

There are three ingredients in the good life: learning, earning, and yearning.
—Christopher Morley, *Parnassus on Wheels*

CHAPTER III
REGIONAL MOVEMENT
OF HUMAN CAPITAL IN THEORY

TREATING HUMAN CAPITAL as a factor of production separate from labor requires a re-examination of the idea of "labor intensive" and "capital intensive" activities, and a reconsideration of the theory of resource movements between regions.

In view of the greatly increased importance of highly trained people in modern economic activity it can be misleading to consider the contribution of the human agent to be that of "labor." About a decade ago "Leontief's paradox" received a great deal of attention in the economic journals. Leontief applied his input-output analysis to American foreign trade and found, paradoxically, that our exports were labor intensive while our imports tended to be capital intensive. A simple explanation of the paradox may be that our statisticians have classified too much of our resources as labor and too little as capital. If the return on personal and social investment in professional, technical, and managerial personnel and in skilled workers were considered to be a return to capital instead of a return to labor, it might well turn out that our imports are, after all, labor intensive and that our exports are capital intensive.[1] Along the same line, Gary Becker has written that students of international trade have been somewhat shaken in recent years by Leontief's findings and by a corroborative finding by Irving Kravis[2] that export industries pay higher wages than import competing industries. Becker states that earnings are gross of the return on human capital and that "export industries might pay higher wages than import competing ones primarily because they employ more skilled or healthier workers."[3] It is evident that re-examination of both the idea and the identity of labor intensive and capital intensive industries is needed. This will be attempted in Chapter 6, particularly for southern manufacturing.

Disregarding, for the moment, human capital as a separate factor of production, a general picture of the needed long run movement of labor and capital to equalize rates of returns between regions is furnished by Figure 1.[4] The marginal value product of southern labor applied to the existing stock of material capital in the region is represented by curve VMP$_s$. Reading instead from right to left, the curve VMP$_n$ represents the value of the marginal product of non-southern labor. This curve is drawn so as to be higher than the other one over most of its range because of the greater amount of material capital per worker in the non-South as a whole.

Current competitive wage rates are determined also by the quantity of labor in the two regions. In the chart, OX represents the number of workers in the South while O'X is the number outside the South. In the absence of net psy-

1. This was pointed out by the present writer in "Human Capital as a Southern Resource," *Southern Economic Journal*, XXIX (January, 1963), 158.

2. Kravis, "Wages and Foreign Trade," *Review of Economics and Statistics*, XXXVIII (February, 1956), 14.

3. Gary S. Becker, "Investment in Human Capital: A Theoretical Analysis," *Journal of Political Economy*, Supplement (October, 1962), p. 44.

4. A similar chart appears in C. L. Allen, J. M. Buchanan, and M. R. Colberg, *Prices, Income, and Public Policy* (New York: McGraw-Hill, 1959), p. 249.

Figure 1 · Regional Labor Productivity

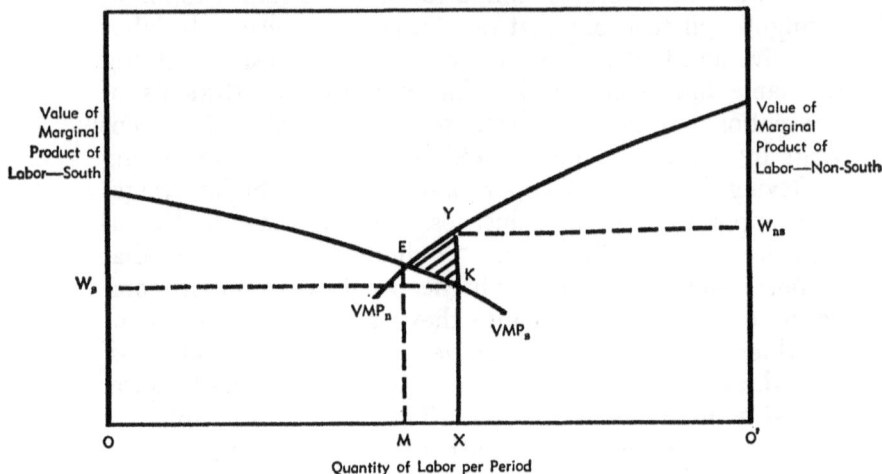

chic incomes or costs attaching to residence in the two regions, MX laborers will have an incentive to leave the South, *ceteris paribus*. (More accurately, the labor input per time period will have to be adjusted by MX.) This would equate money-wage rates in the regions at the level indicated by point E, and the gain in national income per period would be the shaded area EYK. The gain would derive from the better allocation of labor. To the extent the level of the marginal value product curve of southern labor is raised by a southward movement of material capital, a smaller out-migration of labor will be required. Even after full adjustment of resources, however, money wage rates for labor may not be equated since equalizing differences in monetary compensation may be necessary to compensate for non-pecuniary factors such as climate, congestion, urban and rural recreational opportunities, and social attitudes.

REGIONAL SPECIALIZATION AND TRADE

In his pioneering article, Eli Heckscher summarized the prerequisites for initiating international trade as: (1) "different relative scarcity, i.e., different relative prices of the factors of production in the exchanging countries," and (2) "different proportions between the factors of production in different commodities."[5] Heckscher went on to point out that the term "factor of production" does not refer only to broad categories of land, labor, and capital, but to different qualities of each, and that this makes the number of factors almost unlimited. Unfortunately, the use of more than two factors of production makes geometrical and other mathematical models either impossible or quite complex. This led Ohlin to a somewhat looser brand of verbal theorizing in his comprehensive work on the same subject.[6]

The similarity of international trade and inter-regional trade within a given country was emphasized by Ohlin. If we apply the Heckscher-Ohlin approach to the United States economy we are led to the familiar conclusion that the South should specialize in relatively labor-intensive production and the non-South in relatively capital-intensive production. Trade between the regions, a movement of labor out of the South, and a movement of material capital into the South, as just suggested, should tend to equalize absolute real factor returns in the regions. In the case of labor, real returns may be viewed as the sum of money earnings and the monetary equivalent (positive or negative) of psychic factors. For material capital such an adjustment for psychic income or cost is not necessary except in unusual cases. (An owner of an orange grove may derive satisfaction from living next to the grove.)

In a growing, rather than stationary, economy this factor movement would be expected to increase the stock of material capital in the South relative to the rest of the country, probably without causing an absolute decline in capital in the non-South. Similarly, the relative stock of labor in the South would be expected to decline with the passage of time, although the absolute size of the southern labor force

5. Eli Heckscher, "The Effect of Foreign Trade on the Distribution of Income," in Readings in the Theory of International Trade (Philadelphia: The Blakiston Company, 1949), p. 278.

6. Bertil Ohlin, Interregional and International Trade (Cambridge: Harvard University Press, 1935). Ohlin does, however, include a brief mathematical appendix, treating the mutual relationship of prices under simplified conditions.

might not become smaller. What has actually happened in recent years?

MATERIAL CAPITAL

The question is not easy to answer with great confidence because regional estimates of the stock of material capital are available only for manufacturing and only for a few years. Estimates of the total labor force within the conceptual framework of this book require a somewhat arbitrary division of employed persons into those whose services are largely attributable to human capital and those whose services are largely labor. While the latter separation must be rough, it should provide results more meaningful than the alternative of treating both the philosopher and the common street porter as laborers.

The South's share of the nation's manufacturing capital is increasing, according to available data. Between 1954 and 1957 the South Atlantic and East South Central states combined are estimated to have increased their share of this capital from 11.8 per cent to 13.8 per cent.[7] Measurement over a longer time span can be made by using Census of Manufactures data. Value added by manufacture less total payroll in manufacturing gives an approximation to Alfred's Marshall's "quasi-rent"—the gross return to machinery, structures, and other capital goods used. This return must take care of depreciation and interest and it includes profits (positive or negative). Quasi-rent after income taxes is sometimes referred to as cash flow. While it is a measurement of the *annual* contribution of material capital rather than of the total stock of capital, quasi-rent changes should indicate whether there has been a relative movement of manufacturing capital toward the South. That such a movement did occur between 1939 and 1958 is indicated in Table 3-1.

The gain in the South's share of the national total quasi-rent occurred in all three census divisions. Texas, Louisiana, Oklahoma, and Arkansas make up the West South

7. Data are from Lowell E. Gallaway, "Regional Capital Estimates by Industry, 1954-57," *Southern Economic Journal*, XXIX (July, 1962), 24.

TABLE 3-1. SOUTH'S SHARE OF QUASI-RENT ON MANUFACTURING
CAPITAL

Region	1939	1947	1954	1958
South Atlantic	9.7	10.3	9.6	11.0
East South Central	3.7	4.3	4.4	5.0
West South Central	3.8	5.0	5.6	6.4
South	17.2	19.6	19.6	22.4

Source: *1958 Census of Manufactures*, vol. III, *Area Statistics*. See Appendix, Table I, for data from which these percentages were computed.

Central division, which enjoyed the largest gain relative to the country as a whole.

As a group, the South Atlantic states seem to show the smallest relative progress in building their stock of manufacturing capital. Their more spotty progress is indicated also by data on new capital expenditures in manufacturing (including expenditures for replacement of machinery and equipment). Table 3-2 shows capital expenditures in manufacturing industries, as reported by the Bureau of the Census, but expressed again as a percentage of the United States total. (Data are not available for 1939.)

TABLE 3-2. SOUTH'S SHARE OF NEW CAPITAL EXPENDITURES
IN MANUFACTURING (PER CENT OF U.S. TOTAL)

Region	1947	1954	1958
South Atlantic	11.3	10.1	10.9
East South Central	4.3	5.1	5.2
West South Central	7.6	9.2	9.5
South	23.2	24.4	25.6

Source: U.S. Bureau of the Census, *1958 Census of Manufactures*, vol. III, *Area Statistics*. See Table II (Appendix) for data from which these percentages were computed.

For the South as a whole, and for most of the subregions, the share of new capital expenditures exceeds the share of quasi-rents (Tables 3-2 and 3-1, respectively). This indicates that the South's portion of manufacturing quasi-rents will continue to increase beyond 1958. That is, the

35

productive contribution of new manufacturing capital is made chiefly in years subsequent to the year the capital outlay is made. An excess of the percentages in Table 3-2 over those in Table 3-1 suggests an augmented cash flow in future years in the region, relative to the nation as a whole. Much of this increase will occur in the West South Central States.[8]

One source of error in using ratios between comparable percentages in Tables 3-2 and 3-1 as indicators of future progress is the erratic nature of yearly capital expenditures. (Yearly quasi-rents, being based on accumulated stock of manufacturing capital, should be more stable.) Another possible source of error is the inclusion of expenditures for replacement purposes as well as for net expansion of industrial capacity.[9] Nevertheless, for the South as a whole, the persistent and sizeable excess of share of capital expenditures over share of yearly quasi-rents should be a significant indicator of a future rise in the region's share of manufacturing quasi rents.

QUASI-RENTS IN SOUTHERN STATES

Most of the southern states increased their share of the nation's manufacturing capital, as measured by share of annual quasi-rents, between 1939 and 1958. This shows up in Table 3-3, where states are listed in the order of their portion of total United States manufacturing quasi-rent in 1958. The ranking does not necessarily reflect a state's relative importance in manufacturing, since this may be better reflected by value added, but instead reflects the relative importance of the contribution of material capital. In 1958 Texas led by a wide margin, having replaced

8. Ezra Solomon and Zarko Bilbija, in *Metropolitan Chicago* (Glencoe: The Free Press, 1959), p. 92, use a similar comparison on an industry-by-industry basis, between the Chicago metropolitan area's share in U.S. capital expenditures and its share in value added by manufacture. Since the latter includes the contribution of labor and human capital as well as that of material capital, it appears to be desirable to reduce the value-added data to quasi-rents by subtracting payrolls.

9. These and other possible objections to their quite similar measures for Chicago are set forth by Solomon and Bilbija, *ibid.*, p. 93.

TABLE 3-3. QUASI-RENTS IN MANUFACTURING, BY STATE, IN
THE SOUTH (PER CENT OF U.S. TOTAL)

State	1939	1958
Texas	2.14	4.20
North Carolina	2.53	2.43
Virginia	1.92	1.74
Tennessee	1.43	1.70
Maryland	1.79	1.68
Kentucky	0.83	1.61
Georgia	1.17	1.54
Alabama	1.11	1.31
Louisiana	0.96	1.20
Florida	0.51	1.12
West Virginia	0.85	0.97
South Carolina	0.56	0.94
Oklahoma	0.46	0.53
Arkansas	0.28	0.45
Mississippi	0.31	0.43
Delaware	0.21	0.34
District of Columbia	0.16	0.13

Source: U.S. Bureau of the Census, *1958 Census of Manufactures*, vol. III,
Area Statistics. See Table III (Appendix) for data from which percentages were computed.

North Carolina which declined slightly in its percentage of
the national total. Although Florida made an especially
sharp gain, it still did not rank near the top among southern
states in manufacturing in 1958. Omitting the District of
Columbia, only three southern states show a smaller percentage of national quasi-rent in manufacturing in 1958
than prior to World War II. Although progress in building
manufacturing capital was outstanding in Texas, southern
progress on this score is by no means just Texan.

NON-MANUFACTURING CAPITAL MOVEMENTS

Available data also indicate a modest relative movement of agricultural capital toward the South. The value
of farms (land and buildings) increased from 28 per cent
of the national total in 1945 to 30 per cent in 1950 and 1954.
A more rapid relative southern gain in capital invested in

TABLE 3-4.   VALUE OF FARM LAND AND BUILDINGS
($ BILLION)

Region	1945	1950	1954
United States	$46.4	$75.3	$97.6
South	13.1	23.0	29.5
South as % of U.S.	28%	30%	30%

Source: *U.S. Census of Agriculture*, 1954.

farm implements and machinery is suggested by the limited data available.[10] This share rose from 23 per cent in 1940 to 25 per cent in 1945 and to 28 per cent in 1950.

Little information is available on capital in the mineral industries. For census purposes these include mining of metals, coal, and non-metallic minerals, as well as oil and gas extraction. The West South Central states are extremely important, accounting in 1954 and 1958 for over half of the nation's investment in mineral industries, with development and exploration expenditures being especially high. This dominance permitted capital expenditures in the South to increase from 62 to 63 per cent of the nation's capital expenditures in the mineral industries between 1954 and 1958.[11]

Regional data on capital invested in other productive activities are not available, to the writer's knowledge. Those which have been cited indicate a relative gain by the South during World War II and a continued gain during the 1950's.

CHANGES IN SOUTHERN LABOR FORCE

The relative change in the total labor force in the South also seems to be consistent with the Heckscher-Ohlin theory. If we tentatively classify all human productive effort as labor, the South's proportion of all laborers declined

10. A. S. Tostlebe, *The Growth of Physical Capital in Agriculture, 1870-1950* (New York: National Bureau of Economic Research, 1954).

11. Source: U.S. Bureau of the Census, *1958 Census of Mineral Industries*.

from 30.5 of the U.S. total in 1939 to 28.8 per cent of the total in 1959, according to Census of Population data. Heavy outmigration of Negroes during the two decades is reflected in the data of Table 3-5.

TABLE 3-5. SOUTH'S SHARE OF EMPLOYED PERSONS, ALL
OCCUPATIONS (THOUSANDS)

	1939	1949	1959
South	13,778	16,494	18,616
United States	45,166	56,225	64,639
% in South	30.5	29.3	28.8

Source: *U.S. Census of Population,* vol. I, 1940, 1950, and 1960.

Comparison of available figures pertaining to the South's share of the nation's stock of material capital and the figures of Table 3-5 on the region's share of employed persons tends to confirm the idea that the South is still a region with a relative labor surplus (or capital deficiency). However, the needed relative movement of labor and material capital appears to be taking place, with the latter accounting for more of the required adjustment. In general this is a favorable situation since difficult human problems, at least of a short-run nature, are likely to accompany migration. These stresses can be avoided to the extent that capital moves to the people rather than people having to move to the capital.

HUMAN CAPITAL MOVEMENT IN THEORY

The Heckscher-Ohlin theory of trade and resource movements assumes substantial and persistent relative excesses of capital in one region and of labor in another region with which it has economic communication. If human capital is considered to be a separate factor of production, how should it move regionally?

A key assumption in predicting the regional movement of human capital is that there exists at all times a fairly "correct" inter-regional allocation of this resource within the United States due to a high degree of mobility of educated individuals. Consequently, relative surpluses of human capital are unlikely to exist in any region. This contrasts with the situation for ordinary labor, which is relatively abundant in the South, and with material capital, which is relatively abundant in the non-South. Whether human capital should be moving into or out of the South depends on whether it is more highly complementary to labor or to material capital as a factor of production. In the first case human capital should be leaving the South; in the other case it should be following material capital Southward.

Strong complementarity probably exists between material capital and human capital created by means of educational investment in such professional persons as engineers, architects, chemists, plant managers, draftsmen, and accountants. On the other hand, greater complementarity with labor would seem to exist for such professional persons as doctors, nurses, lawyers, social workers, dentists, and teachers. As a consequence, complementarity with "laborers" or their children should be a principal variable in explaining the regional movement of teachers, nurses, and others in this group. Roughly, it may be said that these professional persons should follow the population rather than the material capital.

The greater prevalence of racial segregation in the South during the 1939-1959 period should have important effects on the regional movement of human capital. Since the outmigration of Negroes from the South has been so important in volume, an outflow of human capital embodied in complementary professional persons would be expected. Segregation causes these complementary professionals to be primarily of the same race. The relative movement of colored professional people complementary to material capital would be expected to be in the opposite direction, but probably not strongly. Lack of professional education for material-capital-complementary employment among southern Negroes has often been noted. This lack of training is probably due in part to discrimination by employers in these fields. Also the complementarity of the sexes within the family is probably an important factor. If one professional spouse secures a better position in another region, the other spouse, even if equally educated in another profession, is motivated to move.

These hypotheses with respect to the regional movement of persons embodying much human capital will be tested empirically in subsequent chapters.

Education is the best provision for the journey to old age.

—Aristotle, *Diogenes Lærtius*

CHAPTER IV

THE COLLEGE GRADUATE

AND THE SOUTH

IT IS NOT CORRECT, of course, to imply that all human capital is embodied in persons who hold university degrees. Skills learned in secondary schools, vocational schools, on the job, on athletic fields, and many other places contribute greatly to such capital. Yet college graduates are an example par excellence of persons who embody much human capital, and they appear to be worthy of special attention in the present study. Observed movements of college graduates should be highly correlated with movements of human capital measured in a more sophisticated way. Also, since Census of Population data show a good deal of detail for college graduates, and for the occupations in which they are largely engaged, important additional insights regarding human capital can be gained in this way. Among them are insights related to segregation of the races.

Direct measurement of the migration of college graduates between regions would be useful. Migration measurements are common for the population as a whole and would seem to be reasonably accurate. One method involves using at least two censuses. Each age group counted in a particular region in the earlier census is "looked upon as a set of real cohorts, born in specified years, that pass through time together."[1] A "zero net migration" population for the cohort is found by deducting estimated mortality for the intercensus period. Comparison of this population with the actual number of persons (now 10 years older) in the second census shows net migration for the age group. Positive and negative net migration estimates for all regions in the nation should cancel out except for errors in reporting, errors in estimating mortality, and international immigration affecting the country's population.

In principle the same method might be useful in estimating the interregional migration of college graduates (or persons of any educational status). In practice there has been so much movement between sets of cohorts in the United States that the method is not feasible for the 1939-59 period. Spurred by veterans' educational grants and by the generally increased popularity of education, even persons twenty-five years of age and older have been attending college to such a degree that "migration" out of the 1939 educational cohort tends to swamp migration between regions. The abnormal mortality in the younger age groups during the wars in which the United States was engaged between 1939 and 1959 would also disturb the migration estimates.

The importance of continued education, especially, can be seen in Table 4-1. Column 1 shows the 1939 inventory of men, 25 years and older, with 16 or more years of education, separately for the white and non-white races. Column 2 shows the normal probability of living at least ten more years for each age group. This permits calculation of the number in each age group (now 10 years older) who should still be living in 1949. These "potential populations" in 1949 are shown in Column 3. Actual populations for 1949 are shown in Column 4. The excess of actual over potential

1. Philip M. Hauser and Otis D. Duncan (eds.), *The Study of Population* (Chicago: The University of Chicago Press, 1959), p. 492.

TABLE 4-1. MALE COLLEGE GRADUATES IN THE UNITED STATES—
ACTUAL AND CALCULATED

Age Group	1939 Actual (25-64 years)	Probability of Living in 1949	1949 Potential (35-74 years)	1949 Actual (35-74 years)	1949 Difference (Actual minus Potential)
White					
TOTAL	1,835,001		1,669,899	1,872,260	+202,361
25-29 in 1939	364,710	.980	357,416	430,845	+ 73,429
30-34	362,789	.971	352,268	394,990	+ 42,722
35-44	532,813	.939	500,311	552,070	+ 51,759
45-54	362,154	.855	309,642	330,905	+ 21,263
55-64	212,535	.707	150,262	163,450	+ 13,188
Non-White					
TOTAL	43,254		36,745	50,330	+ 13,585
25-29 in 1939	8,351	.952	7,950	13,130	+ 5,180
30-34	8,049	.930	7,486	10,640	+ 3,154
35-44	12,805	.880	11,268	14,040	+ 2,772
45-54	9,014	.762	6,869	8,290	+ 1,421
55-64	5,035	.630	3,172	4,230	+ 1,058

Source: *U.S. Census of Population,* 1940 and 1950. U.S. Department of Health, Education, and Welfare, Public Health Service, "United States Life Tables, 1949-51," *Vital Statistics and Special Reports,* XLI (Nov., 1954).

population is shown in Column 5. In the main, this probably indicates the gain in the inventory of college graduates due to the receipt subsequent to 1939 of bachelor's degrees by men who were 25 or more in age in that year. Veterans' educational grants were undoubtedly a great factor in the gain in degrees for the younger groups. In addition, immigration of college graduates into the United States after 1939, to the extent that they were 35 years old or older in 1949, would contribute to the gain. It is also likely that the mortality experience for non-white college graduates is more favorable than for non-white men as a whole. However, increased wartime mortality is an offsetting factor.

Table 4-1 suggests that veterans' educational grants were instrumental in building up the stock of non-white college graduates by a larger percentage than the stock of white graduates. This suggests that lack of funds has been a greater obstacle to non-whites so far as college attendance is concerned. Alternatively, the employment opportunities for college-educated non-white men may have increased markedly in the immediate postwar period. In both cases the increase was greatest in the youngest group—20 per cent for whites and 61 per cent for non-whites. The total stock of male college graduates 35 years and older in 1949 was built up by 11 per cent for whites and by 31 per cent for non-whites. In the main this seems to be due to additional education among those who had not yet graduated from college in 1939, since it is clear that favorable mortality experience could not account for a large part of the gain, except in the older age groups. Exaggeration of educational attainment to census takers probably plays a part also since this tends to increase with age and may well be greater for non-whites.

Whatever the relative weights of factors affecting column 5 may have been, it appears to be unfeasible to measure the migration of college graduates in a way comparable to that which is usable for the population as a whole. A further difficulty with the method is that movement of graduates who were younger than 25 in 1939 would not be detected. However, if these persons are included, the migration measurement problem caused by additional schooling is even more serious.

In principle, another way of measuring migration of college graduates involves starting with a census count of all persons with sixteen or more years of schooling, adding new recipients of bachelor's degrees in the state for the next ten-year period, deducting estimated mortality, and comparing this potential population of college graduates with the actual population of such persons in the state shown by the next census. In practice, serious difficulties appear here also. The U.S. Office of Education does not report bachelor's degrees alone, but includes the first professional degree. In a ten-year period, many individuals would be counted twice. Also, many students graduate from institutions in states where they do not intend to remain, so any measurement of the expected number in a state is nebulous on this score. Also, degrees granted non-white students cannot be ascertained for the United States as a whole and are subject to error in the southern states to the extent that segregation in higher education was incomplete. So far as it has appeared feasible to break down the U.S. Office of Education data by race in southern states, Table IV (Appendix) shows the approximate number of degrees earned by whites and non-whites, separately by sex, from 1950-51 through 1957-58. These figures were compiled from data arranged on a school-by-school basis.

The principal source of error in breaking down earned degrees by race in the South probably derives from incomplete segregation in some of the colleges and universities during the period covered. The University of Virginia, for example, had a number of non-white students during the period. Also some white students have attended primarily Negro institutions in the South. These sources of inexactness in the racial breakdown are not believed to distort the data very seriously, but there is probably some understatement of the number of degrees granted to non-whites, the understatement being greater toward the end of the period. It should be noted that the South in Table IV (Appendix) excludes Maryland, Delaware, and the District of Columbia because it cannot be assumed that institutions of higher learning in these states are completely segregated.

Perhaps the most interesting fact which emerges from these data is that non-white female graduates outnumber non-white males. This is the opposite of the situation for white students, since degrees granted white men exceeded those earned by white women by more than two to one. However, over fifty per cent more degrees (bachelor's and first professional) were earned in the South by non-white women than by non-white men during the period 1950 through 1958. The excess of colored female graduates was smaller in 1950-51, due to training of war veterans at government expense, but this influence faded rapidly the next year. A similar powerful trend was evident among white males, and a similar diminution occurred the following year.

Half a century ago approximately three times as many college degrees were granted to non-white men as to non-white women, according to a government survey of predominantly southern colleges.[2] The changed situation during the 1950's is evident in the following percentages computed from Appendix Table IV and from population figures for the same fourteen southern states: (a) The number of non-white males in the South was about 26 per cent of the number of white males in 1959, but non-whites earned only 8 per cent as many degrees as whites during the eight year period; (b) the number of non-white females in the South was about 28 per cent as great as the number of white females while the number of earned degrees was about 26 per cent as great. These comparisons could be made somewhat more accurately (by considering only the college-age population, for example) but they would still tell the same story —non-white men are graduating from college in the South to a much smaller extent than are white men, but non-white women have had almost as good a record as white women.

This comparison of college degrees and population implies that residents of the South attend college in the South. In the main this is true, but the federal survey of Negro education cited above states that to a surprising degree non-white residents of Northern states attended colleges in the South just before World War II. This practice was much more common than that of southern Negroes going to the North for advanced education. Consequently, the ratio of college graduates to total population for southern residents is probably exaggerated in the data of Appendix Table IV. This makes the record appear to be poor indeed for the male non-white population of the South, but still surprisingly good for non-white southern women. It would appear that the lack of job opportunities for non-white college graduates in the South is a greater deterrent to college study among non-white men than is the lack of funds. Permanent income, rather than present income of students or their

2. *National Survey of Higher Education of Negroes* (Washington: Federal Security Agency, U.S. Office of Education, 1942), vol. II, part 1, chapter 1, p. 4.

families, seems largely to determine the supply of college students.

It is interesting to note that the number of degrees granted in the South to non-white women reached a peak around the time of the May 1954 Supreme Court decision outlawing segregated schooling and then declined, with the decline being sharp by 1957. This is probably not accidental, in view of the stimulus given by segregated schooling to the employment of non-white female teachers in the South. On the other hand, employment prospects for college-educated non-white men may have been improved by the Supreme Court decision. Degrees awarded among this group hit a low in 1953-54 and then began to increase markedly.

Outside the South non-white men perhaps attend college to a slightly greater extent than do non-white women, although this is difficult to ascertain because of the greater prevalence of integrated schools and the lack of racial identification in data on degrees granted. Non-white female college graduates in the entire United States in 1959 outnumbered non-white male college graduates by more than 27,000. In the South (census definition) alone, non-white females with four or more years of college education outnumbered similarly educated non-white males by about 42,000. While non-white men residing outside the South appear, consequently, to attend college to a greater extent than do non-white women, the excess is not large. Non-white college graduates who have migrated from the South enter into these data, causing further difficulty in sharpening the picture.

THE SOUTH'S SHARE OF COLLEGE GRADUATES

The idea that graduates of southern universities have to leave the region in order to obtain suitable employment has frequently been discussed. Usually the examples come from college placement officers who have ready access only to a partial picture. Numerous factors tend to limit the value of their observations. First, they can see many instances in which their graduates migrate from the region, but are less likely to be aware of cases in which former graduates move back into the South. Second, they are especially unlikely to detect inmigration of graduates of other universities. As was shown in Chapter 1, in the course of a year a heavy two-way traffic of migrants occurs for every state. Third, officials of universities which are successful in placing most of their students in positions within the state are unlikely to publicize this fact. Bad news usually makes more headlines. This is not to say, however, that some southern states are not investing substantial sums in educating students who will leave the state in greater numbers than other states are educating people for the state in question. This is especially likely to be true with respect to investment in the education of Negroes.

A summary picture of the college graduate population (16 or more years of schooling) is given in Table 4-2. For the South and for the nation as a whole, white males with this much education have gained relative to similarly trained white women. However, non-white women with four or more years of study beyond high school have gone well ahead of non-white men in numbers. Outside the South this is not the case.

When the same type of data are shown for the South as a percentage of the national totals, as in Table 4-3, clearer trends emerge. The region's share of college-educated white males increased markedly in 1949 compared with 1939 and in 1959 compared with 1949. For these men under 25 years of age the proportions of the national totals are considerably higher than for the 25 and over group. It appears that the South as a whole is offering relatively favorable employment opportunities for these young men. However, an increase in the southern share of college-educated men 25 years old and older also occurred during the period.

Little change in the southern portion of college-educated white women shows up. However, some diminution in their relative opportunities in the South may be reflected in the decline in the percentage of young (under 25) white wom-

49

en counted as having southern residence in 1959.

A marked decrease in the relative attractiveness of the South to college-educated non-white men shows up in Table 4-3. For those in the 25 years and over age group, the decline in the region's share was from 52.3 per cent in

TABLE 4-2.   INVENTORY OF COLLEGE GRADUATES, SOUTH AND U.S.
(THOUSANDS)

Year	South				United States			
	White		Non-White		White		Non-White	
	Male	Female	Male	Female	Male	Female	Male	Female
1939*	436	351	24	27	1,975	1,344	46	42
1949	751	552	39	58	2,946	2,162	81	96
1959	1,216	818	70	112	4,803	3,054	176	203

Source: *U.S. Census of Population,* 1940, 1950, 1960.
   * Includes only persons 25 years and older, with 16 or more years of education. Other years include all persons with this amount of schooling.

1939 to 39.7 per cent in 1959. As already indicated, it is difficult to estimate the migration of persons by educational category, but there appears to be little doubt that some thousands of southern non-white men educated in colleges and universities in the region left for more promising opportunities between the 1950 and 1960 census takings. This appears to have been an important human capital export for the South.

The decline in the South's share of all well-educated non-white women has been smaller. For the 25 and over group the region's share fell from 63.95 per cent in 1939 to 55.12 per cent in 1959. An acceleration of the rate of decline is probably underway. The regional proportion of young (under 25) educated non-white women was lower in 1959 than for the older group. This is consistent with the decline in degrees granted to non-white women, as already noted to have occurred since the May 1954 Supreme Court decision outlawing segregated schooling. The employment of non-white female school teachers in the South

TABLE 4-3. SOUTH'S SHARE OF COLLEGE GRADUATES

Group	Year		
	1939	1949	1959
White Males			
Under 25	*	27.48	28.14
25 and over	22.06	23.28	25.11
TOTAL	*	23.59	25.32
White Females			
Under 25	*	27.45	24.88
25 and over	26.10	25.53	26.95
TOTAL	*	25.73	26.78
Non-White Males			
Under 25	*	52.69	40.41
25 and over	52.30	48.96	39.71
TOTAL	*	49.26	39.77
Non-White Females			
Under 25	*	63.82	53.85
25 and over	63.95	59.90	55.12
TOTAL	*	60.46	55.00

Source: *U.S. Census of Population*, 1940, 1950, 1960. Detailed Characteristics by State, and U.S. Summary.
* Not available.

and outside the region will be examined in some detail in Chapter 5.

PROFESSIONAL PERSONS IN THE SOUTH

In spite of the divergent movements for the races, the overall share of the South in the nation's stock of college-educated persons increased—for the 25 and over group —from 24.6 in 1939 to 26.8 per cent in 1959. This occurred despite the decline in the region's share of the nation's population (31.5 in 1939 to 30.7 in 1959) and in total employed persons (30.5 in 1939 to 28.8 in 1959). Evidently the quality of the working force in the South improved. This qualitative change shows up clearly in census data. It has been observed by a census expert that the great majority of college graduates are employed in professional,

TABLE 4-4. SOUTH'S SHARE OF PROFESSIONAL AND MANAGERIAL OCCUPATIONS (SOUTH AS PERCENTAGE OF U.S. EMPLOYMENT IN EACH CATEGORY)

Group	Professional*		Managerial**		Professional and Managerial	
	1939	1959	1939	1959	1939	1959
Whites						
Male	21.7	23.7	24.7	28.6	23.8	26.2
Female	22.9	26.1	24.9	30.1	23.4	27.0
Non-Whites						
Male	63.9	40.7	45.1	35.0	55.0	38.6
Female	79.3	54.5	60.5	47.5	76.4	53.6
All Persons	24.1	25.8	25.1	29.0	24.6	27.1

Source: Calculated from data in *U.S. Census of Population,* vol. I, 1940 and 1960.
* Professional, managerial, and kindred occupations.
** Managers, officials, and proprietors, non-farm.

technical, and kindred occupations or as non-farm managers, officials, and proprietors.[3] In view of the increase in the southern region's share of college graduates one would also anticipate an increase in the region's share of people in these occupations. As shown in Table 4-4 the South's portion of professional, technical, and kindred workers did rise moderately—from 24.1 in 1939 to 25.8 per cent in 1959.

A larger increase occurred in the southern share of managerial personnel. As also shown in Table 4-4, the sharp increases for both male and female white persons more than offset the decline for non-whites. In total professional and managerial employment, the South's share of the national total rose from 24.6 to 27.1 per cent during the two decades. This appears to be a rather strong indication of a relative move of human capital into the region.

Some progress in separating the philosopher from the common street porter may be made by deducting professional and managerial employees from all employees. The separation is only a rough one, of course, since many persons

3. Herman P. Miller, "Annual and Lifetime Income in Relation to Education: 1939-1959," *American Economic Review,* December 1960, p. 970.

classified in these occupations have much less education and skill than many who are classified in other groups. Results of this approach are shown in Table 4-5 ("professional" and "managerial" are used as short designations for the fuller census terms).

TABLE 4-5. SOUTH'S SHARE OF ALL EMPLOYMENT
(THOUSANDS)

Region and Year	All Occupations	Professional	Managerial	All Other Occupations
1939				
United States	45,166	3,345	3,750	38,071
South	13,778	807	941	12,030
South as % of U.S.	30.5	24.1	25.1	31.6
1949				
United States	56,225	4,909	5,018	46,298
South	16,494	1,236	1,326	13,932
South as % of U.S.	29.3	25.2	26.4	30.1
1959				
United States	64,639	7,232	5,410	51,997
South	18,616	1,862	1,569	15,185
South as % of U.S.	28.8	25.8	29.0	29.2

Source: U.S. Census of Population, vol. I, 1940, 1950, 1960.

The percentages in the right-hand column of Table 4-5 may be considered roughly to reflect the relative use of "labor" in the South during the last three years in which the census was taken. The decline from 31.6 to 29.2 per cent was due principally to outmigration of relatively poorly educated Negroes. Although such relative outmigration occurred also for Negroes in the professional and managerial categories, this was not enough to offset the gain in employment of white people in these categories.

For both men and women, the decline in relative southern employment of Negroes in professional and managerial capacities was greater than the decline in the southern share of college graduates. A great many Negro men in the South are classified as clergymen, and it is likely that relatively few are college graduates. It is probable that many of these men drop out of the professional, technical, and kindred classification when they leave the South. Large numbers of the professional Negro women in the South are classified as nurses (e.g., 15 per cent in Texas in 1959) and the numbers who hold college degrees are certainly much smaller. For both whites and non-whites (but to a greater degree for the latter) a better measure of human capital movement can be devised by considering persons with 16 or more years of schooling than by considering occupations as classified by the Bureau of the Census.

In any case it appears that human capital embodied in white persons has been complementary to material capital and that both have gained in importance in the region since 1939. Although the South's share of all white persons remained nearly stationary at a little over 27 per cent in 1939, 1949, and 1959, the proportion of both the nation's stock of white college graduates and of professional and managerial persons increased.

As will be shown in the next chapter, segregated schooling in the South has been a very favorable factor in the employment of educated Negro women. For the educated male southern Negro this has been a much less important, though not insubstantial, factor. College educated Negro men have not been complementary to manufacturing capital to a degree sufficient to provide much incentive toward staying in the South. This situation appears to be the result both of discrimination in employment and the lack of preparation of non-white men for positions as physical scientists, accountants, managers, and other capital-complementary occupations.

Ivrything that's worth havin' goes to th' city; th' counthry takes what's left.
                    —Finley Peter Dunne,
                    "The City as a Summer Resort"

CHAPTER V
SEGREGATION
AND THE TEACHING PROFESSION

ONE OF THE most emotion-evoking topics of the day is the question of integration or segregation of the races in southern (and northern) schools. At the time of this writing integration is proceeding at a highly uneven pace in the South—rapidly in some places and not at all in others. Paradoxically, the schools of many northern cities are almost as segregated as those of southern cities either through deliberate policy or because of the residential patterns that have evolved.[1] In some cities difficult and costly transpor-

1. Milton Friedman, in *Capitalism and Freedom* (Chicago: University of Chicago Press, 1963), chap. VII, says that in fact much segregation exists in Chicago schools. Recently there have been demonstrations in protest of *de facto* school segregation in Boston, St. Louis, and other cities.

According to the *Wall Street Journal,* July 31, 1963, p. 1, one out of every two New York City elementary schools is either 90% or more white or just as heavily Negro and Puerto Rican; nearly one fourth of the Philadelphia schools are 99% or more white or Negro; in Baltimore 27% of the white students and 41% of the Negro students attend fully segregated schools.

tation of pupils to and from non-neighborhood schools is being resorted to as a means of forcing desegregation.

The present writer will not set forth a value judgment in this field. However, the continued existence of largely segregated education in the South has important implications for the chief subject under investigation, namely, human capital and its regional movement, and these implications can be examined objectively from an economic viewpoint. (The viewpoint is positive rather than normative.) Similarly, the economic implications of desegregation in education can be assessed, especially with the aid of data from the Census of Population. Special attention will be focused on the non-white female school teacher since the teaching profession is unique in the opportunity it (sometimes) affords college-educated non-white women for relatively remunerative employment.

SEGREGATION AND EDUCATIONAL INPUTS

Racial segregation among pupils, especially when supported by local law, is usually accompanied by employment of a teacher of the same race. A very strong complementarity then exists between students (who are a sort of raw material) and teachers (whose services are primarily those of immaterial capital). Inputs of students and teachers of the same race are almost in fixed proportions except for the possibility of varying the student-teacher ratio from school to school. A higher ratio tends to reduce the cost of production of education but at a sacrifice in quality of output.

In a state with a completely segregated school system one would expect the proportion of non-white teachers to approximate the percentage of non-white pupils in the school age population. Equality of employment opportunity for members of the two principal races to hold teaching positions in proportion to their numbers is promoted by segregation, by equality of student-teacher ratios, and by compulsory and voluntary school attendance in equal degree on the part of the school age population.[2] "Equality" in this respect does not imply lack of discrimination in remuneration—a matter which will be examined later in this chapter.

The northern states[3] have provided far fewer teaching positions to non-whites in proportion to non-white population than have the southern states. This may be seen in Table 5-1. For all of the southern states, and for the northern states where 1960 census data are available in sufficient detail, the table shows percentage of the population from 6 through 18 years of age that was non-white and also the per cent of all elementary and high school teachers that were non-white. The ratio of the second percentage to the first is also shown. This provides an index of employment opportunity, with 1.00 representing full "equality." As indicated above, the ratio is affected by non-attendance on the part of the school-age population and by average class size as well as by the hiring policies of school officials.

Viewed in this way, the employment opportunity of non-white teachers was better in every southern state than in any northern state except Missouri. (And Missouri is often treated as a southern state in regional studies.) Texas, Alabama, Florida, North Carolina, Tennessee, and Virginia most nearly provided full equality of employment opportunity according to this measure. Least equality of opportunity among the northern states shown occurs in South Dakota, Nebraska, Iowa, Connecticut, Wisconsin, and Massachusetts.

While the "better" record of the South in this respect is largely due to the prevalence of the institution of segregated schooling, the record of the Northern states is rather surprisingly poor. Since most teachers are hired by public authorities it is apparent that a great deal of discrimination

2. South Carolina had the highest rural pupil-teacher ratio for Negroes of all of the southern states in 1956-57 according to *Southern Schools: Progress and Problems* (Nashville: Southern Education Reporting Service, 1959), p. 44.

3. "Northern states" are here defined to include New England, Middle Atlantic, East North Central, and West North Central states. However, separate census data for non-white teachers are not available for all of these states.

TABLE 5-1. RELATIVE EMPLOYMENT OF NON-WHITE TEACHERS, 1959

Southern States	(1) Per cent Non-White School Age Population	(2) Per cent Non-White Teachers	(3) Ratio Col. (2) to Col. (1)	Northern States	(4) Per cent Non-White School Age Population	(5) Per cent Non-White Teachers	(6) Ratio Col. (5) to Col. (4)
Alabama	34.4	32.6	.95	Connecticut	4.7	0.9	.19
Arkansas	25.4	20.4	.80	Illinois	11.3	5.7	.50
Delaware	14.8	11.3	.76	Indiana	6.1	3.2	.52
Florida	20.9	19.1	.91	Iowa	1.1	0.2	.18
Georgia	32.5	28.4	.87	Kansas	4.8	2.1	.44
Kentucky	7.7	5.0	.65	Massachusetts	2.5	0.7	.28
Louisiana	36.2	31.1	.86	Michigan	9.8	4.0	.41
Maryland	18.8	16.0	.85	Minnesota	1.3	0.4	.31
Mississippi	48.7	39.5	.81	Missouri	9.9	7.2	.73
North Carolina	30.2	28.2	.93	Nebraska	2.8	0.5	.18
Oklahoma	11.3	6.8	.60	New Jersey	9.2	4.3	.47
South Carolina	41.6	34.6	.83	New York	9.0	2.9	.32
Tennessee	17.6	15.8	.90	Ohio	8.4	3.7	.44
Texas	13.2	12.7	.96	Pennsylvania	8.2	3.8	.46
Virginia	23.3	20.7	.89	South Dakota	5.2	0.8	.15
West Virginia	5.3	4.6	.87	Wisconsin	2.5	0.6	.24

Source: Computed by author from data in U.S. Census of Population: 1960, Detailed Characteristics. Final Report PC(1)2D–52D, Tables 94 and 124.

in employment against non-whites occurs and is carried out by government in the non-South. In no small measure the discrimination is private in nature also since more than 20 per cent of the white students in Wisconsin, Illinois, Pennsylvania, New York, and Massachusetts attend private schools, according to the 1960 Census of Population.

Figure 2 · Non-White Teacher Employment Related to Non-White School Age Population

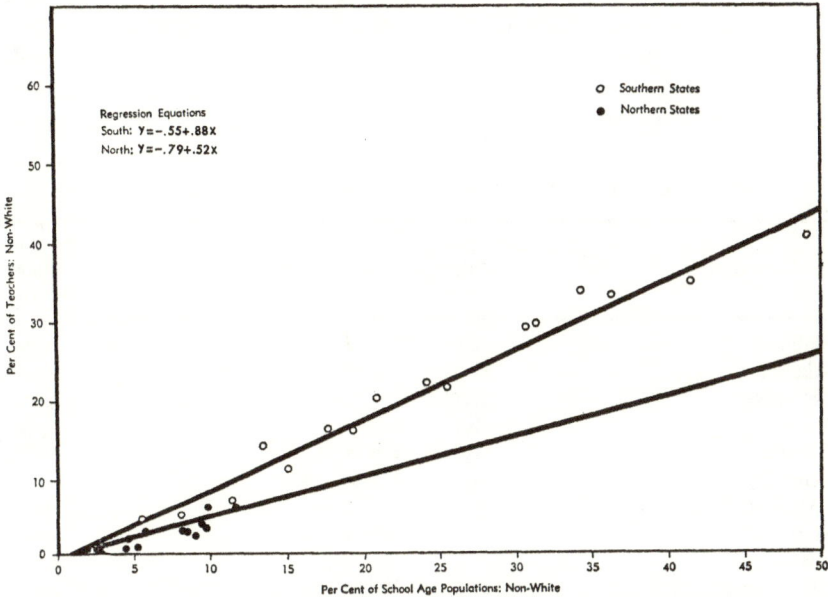

The employment of non-white teachers in relation to non-white school age population is reflected also in Figure 2. Least-squares regressions have been fitted separately for southern and northern states. In both cases the correlation is high. However, the regression line for the South has a much steeper slope. According to the regression equations, a one per cent difference in the non-white school age population was related to a 0.88 per cent difference (in the same direction) in the number of non-white elementary and high school teachers employed in the South. In the northern states a one per cent greater non-white school age population was related to a 0.52 per cent greater employment of non-white teachers. Employment discrimination against non-whites in openly segregated schools has been much smaller than in legally integrated (but often actually segregated) schools. This inference is based on the assumption that there is no large deficiency in the supply of suitably trained non-white teachers in the North.

As would be expected, the southern states hire a smaller percentage of male teachers at the elementary and high school levels than do the northern states. This is shown in Table 5-2. The unweighted average percentage of male teachers was about 29 in the North and about 24 in the South in 1959. In part, at least, this can be explained as

TABLE 5-2. RELATIVE EMPLOYMENT OF MALE TEACHERS, 1959

Southern States	Per cent Male Teachers	Northern States	Per cent Male Teachers
Alabama	20.7	Connecticut	29.9
Arkansas	25.3	Illinois	27.7
Delaware	31.7	Indiana	33.3
Florida	26.7	Iowa	25.9
Georgia	19.8	Kansas	29.8
Kentucky	24.0	Massachusetts	30.4
Louisiana	23.0	Michigan	29.5
Maryland	26.3	Minnesota	30.9
Mississippi	22.2	Missouri	24.8
North Carolina	21.6	Nebraska	23.5
Oklahoma	30.7	New Jersey	28.6
South Carolina	18.9	New York	29.6
Tennessee	22.4	Ohio	27.1
Texas	25.5	Pennsylvania	32.4
Virginia	19.4	South Dakota	29.2
West Virginia	27.1	Wisconsin	28.5
Average (unweighted)	24.1		28.8

Source: Computed by author from data in U.S. *Census of Population:* 1960, *Detailed Characteristics*, Final Report PC(1)2D-52D.

an economy measure, since the cost of female teachers is lower. For the United States as a whole, 1959 median earnings of male teachers at the high school level were $5,827 compared with $4,427 for female teachers at this level. Men teaching in the elementary schools earned $5,200 compared with $4,033 for women.[4]

It is probable that differences in the pay of male and female teachers is due primarily to the better alternatives of the former. That is, the demand-supply situation is more favorable for the men. Not only is this true at any given level of education at which teachers are employed but these forces work also to cause a concentration of male teachers at the higher levels of schooling. The same census table shows that almost two-thirds of the men are teaching in high schools while only about one-sixth of the women are working at the high school level.

At the time of this writing, national legislation is being written to require "equal pay for equal work" for the two sexes. Salary schedules in most of the school systems which have any schedule at all now call for the same rate of pay for men and women.[5] This is the sort of principle of remuneration that tends to secure wide support but carries hidden dangers. Since alternative employment opportunities for men are usually better than for women, the effect of these salary schedules has undoubtedly been to keep a great many men out of primary and secondary education.

Salary differentials above the amounts in the salary schedule are not an uncommon way to grant "extra pay for extra work." Differentials for a high school "activities manager," athletic coach, debate coach, dramatic coach, or publication adviser can range from $175 to $1000 or more per year.[6] Such differentials are more common at the high school level and go more often to men than to women, thus helping to explain the difference between yearly earnings of the sexes. To some extent these additional payments may properly be regarded as an attempt of the price system to overcome inappropriate salary schedules. An increase

4. *U.S. Census of Population: 1960.* Vol. I, *Characteristics of the Population,* Part 1, United States Summary, Table 208, p. 555.

5. S. J. Knezevich and J. G. Fowlkes, *Business Management of Local School Systems* (New York: Harper and Row, 1960), p. 77.

6. *Ibid.,* p. 79.

in side payments and fringe benefits of a great many kinds to men, and increased unemployment among women, may confidently be expected to be a consequence of national legislation requiring equal pay for equal work for the two sexes. Such legislation bears a strong kinship to minimum wage laws, which have the effect of reducing the relative employment of the least productive workers.

TEACHERS' SALARIES

It has often been pointed out that teachers' salaries are lower on the average in the South than outside the region. During the 1956-57 school year, for example, the average annual salary in sixteen southern states (including Missouri and excluding Texas) was reported to be $3,438 compared with $4,220 for the nation as a whole.[7] It has also been pointed out that the gap between salaries of white and non-white teachers in the South has been greatly reduced.

> Before the 1940's, the differences between salaries of white and Negro teachers in the South were less a measure of qualification than of official discrimination. Individual variations in training, tenure and experience have persisted, but as more money has become available for education, and as school equalization has progressed, the salaries of Negro teachers have closely approached those of white teachers similarly qualified. One or two states, in fact, are paying more on the average to Negroes than to whites.[8]

A statistical tabulation showing average annual salaries separately by race and by rural and metropolitan residence showed largest salary advantages for white compared with non-white teachers to exist in Mississippi, both rural and urban.[9] Higher average salary payments to Negro teachers were shown for urban Alabama, both rural and urban North Carolina, rural Tennessee, and both rural and urban Virginia. In all other cases white teachers received higher salaries.

7. *Southern Schools: Progress and Problems,* p. 141.
8. Ernst W. Swanson and John A. Griffin, *Public Education in the South* (Chapel Hill: University of North Carolina Press, 1955), p. 58.
9. *Southern Schools: Progress and Problems,* p. 144.

While increasing recognition has been given to the need to separate urban and rural residence in order properly to compare teachers' salaries, it has not been done with sufficient care in most of the studies which have come to the writer's attention. These studies often have the further disadvantage of including both male and female teachers in the average salary computations. The present chapter will emphasize the salaries of female teachers only, in order to eliminate this variable. Also, there is need to treat urban or rural residence carefully. A fairly good way to handle this important variable appears to be to measure for each state the proportion of the actual school population (rather than school-age population) classified by the Bureau of the Census as living in urban places in 1959. Presumably this is also a good measure of the proportion of urban teachers in a state. This variable is shown in Table 5-3 separately for the white and non-white population of sixteen southern states and District of Columbia and for seventeen northern states. (Western states and northern states with small non-white populations are omitted.)

Quite a remarkable concentration of the non-white population in cities shows up in the North. However, in Mississippi and South Carolina, as well as in the Dakotas, the non-white population is less urban than is the white population. In many southern states there is little difference in this respect between the races.

If the earnings of female school teachers as shown in Table 5-4 are taken by themselves, they suggest that there is a substantial discrimination against white teachers in both the North and South! Eleven northern states paid more to non-white women, while five paid more to white women. In the South, ten states paid more to non-white and six paid more to white women.[10] These census data reflect earnings from all sources rather than salaries. However, rentier income of teachers is usually very modest. Also, yearly earnings data have the advantage of reflecting the amount of employment actually provided while yearly

10. The District of Columbia, which is a special case, and North Dakota, where comparable data are not available, are eliminated from this comparison.

TABLE 5-3. PER CENT OF SCHOOL POPULATION WITH URBAN RESIDENCE, 1959

Southern States	White	Non-White	Northern States	White	Non-White
Alabama	51.0	52.7	Connecticut	75.6	95.9
Arkansas	37.9	39.8	Illinois	76.9	98.2
Delaware	65.9	61.1	Indiana	58.4	97.5
District of Columbia	100.0	100.0	Iowa	48.4	95.3
Florida	70.9	74.2	Kansas	59.0	91.4
Georgia	51.6	52.8	Massachusetts	81.8	92.1
Kentucky	38.2	70.4	Michigan	68.5	96.0
Louisiana	60.9	57.8	Minnesota	59.0	70.1
Maryland	71.4	76.0	Missouri	62.0	89.6
Mississippi	38.4	27.7	Nebraska	50.3	84.5
North Carolina	36.6	34.7	New Jersey	87.8	91.3
Oklahoma	60.4	58.7	New York	81.1	96.8
South Carolina	43.2	30.0	North Dakota	32.4	13.6
Tennessee	45.5	69.1	Ohio	68.6	95.9
Texas	74.5	72.1	Pennsylvania	66.9	95.4
Virginia	54.2	49.9	South Dakota	38.6	16.9
West Virginia	32.4	42.2	Wisconsin	60.8	85.6

Source: *U.S. Census of Population:* 1960. Vol. I, *Characteristics of the Population,* by state, Table 46.

salary rates may be misleading for substitute teachers.

The principal explanation for the apparent discrimination in salaries against white female school teachers is found in the tendency of the non-white population to concentrate in urban areas. This concentration is apparent in Table 5-3. A strong positive correlation between median earnings of female teachers in a state and the proportion of urban school-age population shows up in Figure 3. (The coefficient of correlation is 0.71, and the chance that no correlation exists is only one in a hundred.) The slope of the regression line indicates a gain of about $26 per year in earnings for each one per cent greater proportion of the school population with urban residence.

It is probable that *real* earnings of urban school teachers do not exceed those of rural teachers by as much as this correlation suggests. Higher land and transportation costs

TABLE 5-4. MEDIAN EARNINGS OF FEMALE SCHOOL TEACHERS, 1959
(DOLLARS PER YEAR)

Southern States	White	Non-White	Northern States	White	Non-White
Alabama	3,334	3,376	Connecticut	5,067	6,499
Arkansas	3,040	2,807	Illinois	4,454	5,182
Delaware	4,858	4,965	Indiana	4,393	4,827
District of Columbia	5,609	5,468	Iowa	3,580	2,100
Florida	4,275	4,418	Kansas	3,751	4,332
Georgia	3,449	3,447	Massachusetts	4,653	3,818
Kentucky	2,797	3,505	Michigan	4,560	5,290
Louisiana	4,420	3,903	Minnesota	3,943	3,550
Maryland	4,638	4,985	Missouri	3,501	4,871
Mississippi	3,333	2,495	Nebraska	3,112	4,500
North Carolina	3,852	3,725	New Jersey	4,978	4,579
Oklahoma	4,305	4,415	New York	5,107	4,951
South Carolina	3,235	2,933	North Dakota	3,301	n.a.
Tennessee	3,254	3,423	Ohio	4,256	4,769
Texas	3,970	4,478	Pennsylvania	4,485	4,604
Virginia	3,590	3,758	South Dakota	2,953	3,750
West Virginia	3,439	3,827	Wisconsin	3,657	4,350

Source: *U.S. Census of Population: 1960, Detailed Characteristics.* Final Report,
PC(1)2D-52D. Table 124.

are usually associated with urban residence. On the other
hand certain advantages traceable to economies of scale in
the provision of consumer goods and services attach to
urban residence. A difficult further problem in assessing
the data is that of quality differences, since the most able
teachers are believed to prefer urban residence on the
average. However, it frequently happens that extremely
capable people prefer to "get away from it all" and to live
even in wilderness areas where they may provide excellent
teaching indeed for a small number of pupils.[11]

11. The National Education Association *Research Bulletin*, XXI (February, 1953), states that rural teachers in 1951-52 had the least amount of
preparation for the job they are trying to do. The bulletin also points
out that the smallest schools and the smallest school districts "have the
least money per classroom unit, the greatest number of unsatisfactory
buildings and the most inadequate equipment."

Figure 3 · Urbanization and Earnings

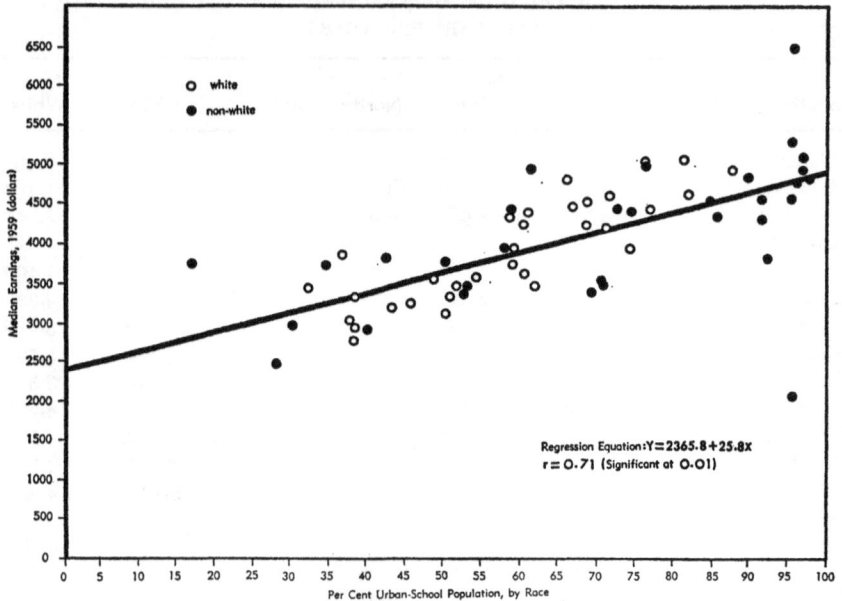

ARE EARNINGS LOWER IN THE SOUTH?

The positive correlation between extent of urban residence and teachers' earnings should be taken into account in measuring regional and racial differences in these earnings. Expected earnings can be calculated from the regression equation represented by the least-squares line fitted to the data in Figure 3. This serves to eliminate the effect of degree of urbanization of a state on female teachers' earnings in that state. Deviations of actual from calculated earnings are shown in Table 5-5.

One way to determine how southern earnings compare with northern earnings—after adjustment for degree of urbanization—is to count the number of positive and negative deviations in Table 5-5. On this basis no difference appears between the regions. In each case there are as many positive as negative deviations. Some deviations are, of course, applicable to large numbers of teachers while others are found from a small number of cases. As a consequence, it is more meaningful to weight each deviation by the number

TABLE 5-5. DEVIATIONS OF ACTUAL FROM CALCULATED EARNINGS*
(DOLLARS PER YEAR)

Southern States	White	Non-White	Northern States	White	Non-White
Alabama	—348	— 349	Connecticut	+751	+1659
Arkansas	—304	— 586	Illinois	+104	+ 283
Delaware	+782	+1023	Indiana	+520	— 54
Florida	+ 80	+ 138	Iowa	— 35	—2725
Georgia	—248	— 281	Kansas	—137	— 392
Kentucky	—554	— 677	Massachusetts	+177	— 924
Louisiana	+483	+ 46	Michigan	+427	+ 447
Maryland	+430	+ 658	Minnesota	+ 55	— 624
Mississippi	— 24	— 585	Missouri	—464	+ 194
North Carolina	+542	+ 464	Nebraska	—552	— 46
Oklahoma	+381	+ 535	New Jersey	+347	— 142
South Carolina	—251	— 207	New York	+649	+ 88
Tennessee	—286	— 726	Ohio	+120	— 71
Texas	—318	+ 252	Pennsylvania	+393	— 223
Virginia	—174	+ 105	South Dakota	—409	+ 948
West Virginia	+237	+ 372	Wisconsin	—277	— 224

* Actual 1959 median earnings of female teachers subtracted from earnings calculated from regression formula of Figure 3.

of teachers in that category and to compute an average deviation per person. These are shown in Table 5-6.

TABLE 5-6. AVERAGE DEVIATION OF EARNINGS FROM EXPECTED
EARNINGS—FEMALE SCHOOL TEACHERS, 1959

Region	White Teachers	Non-White Teachers
Northern States	+$239	+$56
Southern States	— 60	— 65

This calculation shows that median earnings of white female school teachers in the North were about $300 per year more than in the South, after adjustment for extent of urban residence. The actual (unadjusted) difference was almost $700 per year, as noted earlier. After adjustment for urbanization, median earnings of non-white female teachers were only a little more than $100 a year higher in the North than in the South. Here the adjustment for urbanization is especially important, since the actual differential in favor of non-white teachers in the North was more than $1200 per year compared with the same group in the South. In short, non-white female teachers in the primary and secondary grades receive higher pay in the North mainly because they are in the cities rather than because they are in the North.

IS SALARY DISCRIMINATION GREATER IN THE SOUTH?

The data of Table 5-6 seem also to provide a reasonable basis for measuring the average amount of racial discrimination in pay of female teachers of the two races.

The actual weighted median earnings of white female teachers in the North in 1959 were $4416 compared with $4874 for non-white female teachers. This suggests a rather important amount of salary discrimination against the *white* teachers. The same average for southern states were $3744 for white female teachers and $3621 for non-whites. Some discrimination against *non-whites* seems to be suggested.

However, the data of Table 5-6, where the effect of degree of urbanization has been eliminated, show a rather different picture. On the average the northern states discriminated against non-white teachers to a moderate degree—$183 per year. In the South there was almost no discrimination on the average, the difference being $5 per year. The importance of the adjustment is much greater in the North where non-whites are concentrated in the cities of the more populous states, than in the South where there is little difference, on the average, between white and non-white people so far as a revealed preference for urban living is concerned.

When "urbanization adjusted" data are examined on a state-by-state basis a more revealing picture of salary discrimination emerges. Deviations shown in Table 5-5 are usually in the same direction—that is, both are usually negative in low salary states and positive in high salary states. Nevertheless, a substantial difference in the white and non-white deviation for a state may indicate discrimination (relative urbanization having been allowed for).[12]

If a difference in deviations of $400 a year is taken as "substantial," it follows that substantial discrimination in pay against non-white female school teachers occurred in Mississippi, Louisiana, and Tennessee among southern states. In Texas substantial discrimination against white female teachers occurred. In Tennessee non-white female teachers actually had higher median earnings than did whites, so "discrimination" means only that non-white teachers did not enjoy as great an urban salary advantage as usually exists. (It may be noted in Table 5-3 that the non-white school population in Tennessee is much more urban than is the comparable white population.)

The same calculation shows substantial salary discrimination against non-white teachers to be more common in the North than in the South. Iowa, Massachusetts, Minnesota, Pennsylvania, New York, and New Jersey appeared in 1959 to discriminate substantially in salary against non-white female teachers.

Among the northern states substantial salary discrimination against *white* female school teachers appeared to take place in Connecticut, South Dakota, and Nebraska. (Absolute numbers of non-white teachers are small in these states, however, decreasing the importance of median earnings and increasing the possibility of significant distortion of census data through reporting errors.)

SUMMARY

Most of the North-South differential in teachers' median earnings in 1959 disappears when the effects of the greater proportion of male teachers in the North and of greater urbanization in that region are removed. Also, the higher earnings of non-white teachers in many states can be

12. This statement assumes that those who employ teachers believe that the efficiency of the races is the same. Otherwise pay differentials may reflect differences in estimated productivity and these estimates may either be accurate or be distorted by ignorance. See Becker, *Economics of Discrimination,* p. 8, for a discussion of these considerations.

explained by their strong revealed preference for urban living. It is quite possible, in fact, that the *entire* northern advantage in female teachers' salaries can be attributed to greater urban concentration. The adjustment for urbanization which it was possible to make in the present chapter is based only on an urban-rural separation. If comparable data were available it would be better to incorporate city size into the adjustment. A recent publication of the National Education Association[13] shows salaries of teachers according to size of school district. A median salary of $6,359 was reported for school districts with 2500 or more teachers compared with $4,591 for school districts with 1 to 49 teachers. (It was also reported that only 9.7 per cent of the former against 26 per cent of the latter lacked bachelor's degrees.) The NEA publication also shows an advantage of almost $1,000 per year in average salary paid in the largest school districts compared with the next largest districts. The data are not broken down by race, however, and are only partially shown separately for men and women.

That a further adjustment for city size would serve to reduce the northern female teacher earnings advantage shown in Table 5-6 is suggested by the data in Table 5-7. Mississippi and Arkansas, for example, with their small big-city populations would show up to less disadvantage. To a somewhat lesser extent, such northern states as Iowa, Kansas, and Nebraska would also show a better record.

Racial discrimination in salaries paid female school teachers does not loom as very significant, on the average. To the extent such discrimination existed in 1959 against non-white teachers it was more common and greater in amount in the North than in the South.

The earnings data as analyzed in this chapter appear to be inconsistent with one hypothesis set forth by Gary Becker in his well-known book, *The Economics of Discrimination*. Becker states (p. 64): "In Northern states, on the other hand, discrimination by government would be much less, since Negroes do vote, the desire for *government* discrimination is not keen, and race relations is a much less im-

13. *The American School Teacher, 1960-61*, National Education Association Research Monograph 1963-M2, April, 1963.

TABLE 5-7.   PER CENT OF POPULATION LIVING IN STANDARD
METROPOLITAN AREAS, 1959

Southern States	Per cent	Northern States	Per cent
Alabama	45	Connecticut	77
Arkansas	19	Illinois	76
Delaware	68	Indiana	48
Florida	65	Iowa	33
Georgia	46	Kansas	37
Kentucky	34	Massachusetts	85
Louisiana	50	Michigan	73
Maryland	78	Minnesota	51
Mississippi	8	Missouri	57
North Carolina	24	Nebraska	37
Oklahoma	43	New Jersey	78
South Carolina	32	New York	85
Tennessee	45	Ohio	69
Texas	63	Pennsylvania	77
Virginia	50	South Dakota	32
West Virginia	30	Wisconsin	46
Unweighted Averages	44		60

Source: *U.S. Census of Population: 1960*, U.S. Summary, Figure 36, p. 529.

portant issue." This is not to say that Becker's hypothesis would not be consistent with data on government employment outside the teaching field.

Much more important than salary discrimination in teaching is discrimination in employment. Here the 1959 record of the South is much better than that of the North, due of course to openly segregated education. The actual number of non-white elementary and high school teachers (both men and women) in the South in 1959 was about 92,000 according to the census count. If the South hired non-white teachers in proportion to non-white school-attending population only to the extent the North did, this number would have been about 55,000. It follows that about 37,000 teaching jobs for non-whites were traceable to the higher propensity of the South to hire Negroes because of the attempt to maintain segregated schools. The writer does not mean to imply southern virtue or special generosity in setting forth these estimates. Rather, they are meant to be an objective interpretation of the facts as revealed by the 1960 Census of Population.

The implications of the foregoing are rather clear so far as the prospects for use of human capital are concerned. If the South, in the face of federally enforced integration of schools, should move rapidly toward the revealed northern hiring practices for teachers, thousands of Negro teachers will be replaced as soon as acceptable white teachers become available. Sharp increases in the number of white students, especially females, enrolled in schools of education in southern universities will occur along with a drastic decrease in the number of Negro women preparing for a career in education. (This movement appears, in fact, to have been underway at a moderate rate since 1954, according to the estimates of degrees earned by race, which appears in Appendix Table IV.) An adverse effect will also be felt by non-white university professors.

About 60 per cent of all non-white "professional, technical, and kindred" workers in the South in 1959 were elementary and high school teachers. In the northern states about 20 per cent of the same group were employed as teachers, according to census data. Assuming that the end of legal segregation in southern schools will cause the southern states to move a part of the way toward the demonstrated northern practices, a poorer use of educated Negroes from a national point of view is in prospect. Teaching positions lost in the South cannot readily be regained by individuals through migration unless northern states sharply modify their hiring practices. Displaced Negro teachers are not likely often to be highly qualified for other types of professional work, especially to the extent that they have concentrated on "teaching methods" in college. If they are not hired by northern schools as teachers, much of their specialized training will be wasted. Implications for personal hardship and social inefficiency in resource use are clear.

Racial segregation in schooling has been like a protective tariff for the southern non-white teacher, holding down competition strongly and providing a sort of monopoly advantage. When any high tariff wall is taken down a difficult period of adjustment ensues. This is not to say that such walls should not be dismantled. However, the extent of the necessary adjustment, and the consequent advantages of gradualism, seem to have been more clearly recognized by social scientists in the tariff case than in the case of racial desegregation in schooling.[14]

14. The problem of religiously-segregated schools has not been well explored by social scientists. Problems of quality of instruction, discrimination in pay, and discrimination in hiring (including racial discrimination as a by-product) may well be greater between religiously-segregated and unsegregated schools than between those segregated and unsegregated on a racial basis.

The cricket's gone, we only hear machines;
In erg and atom they exact their pay.
And life is largely lived on silver screens,
And chemistry anneals the common clay.
                    —David McCord,
                    Ballads of Time and Space

CHAPTER VI
PROFESSIONAL WORKERS
IN SOUTHERN MANUFACTURING

VICTOR FUCHS' recent study of changes in the location of manufacturing points out that for the 1929-54 period all three census divisions of the South recorded comparative gains in employment and value added by manufacture, but that the pattern of gains varied markedly between these divisions.[1] Fuchs shows that the relative gain of the South Atlantic region was achieved mainly in textiles and that this was a result of the favorable labor situation for this labor-intensive activity. He found that natural resources became more important as an attraction to industry in the East South Central states and most important in the West South Central division.

Similarly, Perloff, Dunn, Lampard and Muth have shown that the Southeast gained sharply in its share of the textiles and apparel industries between 1939 and 1954.[2]

1. Victor Fuchs, *Changes in the Location of Manufacturing in the United States Since 1929* (New Haven and London: Yale University Press, 1962), p. 23.
2. H. Perloff, E. Dunn, E. Lampard, and R. Muth, *Regions, Resources and Economic Growth* (Baltimore: Johns Hopkins Press, 1960), pp. 416-24.

In both cases the attraction of lower-cost labor was deemed to be the major factor in the gain. Where style is of particular importance, however, the older regions have had more success in retaining their share of apparel manufacturing, according to these economists. Miami, Florida, has developed considerably in recent years as a style center and has attracted many apparel firms. However, a recent survey of location factors for the State as a whole indicated that "availability of labor" was more important than "access to market" for the apparel plants locating in Florida in 1956 and 1957.[3]

CAPITAL AND LABOR INTENSIVENESS

If labor and material capital are considered to be the two factors of production, attempts to measure the labor intensiveness of an industry may quite naturally take the form of estimating the amount of such capital per worker. Where the amount is relatively high the industry has been regarded as capital intensive in nature and where it is relatively low as labor intensive. Perloff and his associates, using this calculation, found that the following may be identified as labor intensive: electrical machinery, other machinery, printing, textiles, lumber, furniture, transportation equipment except motor vehicles, leather, and apparel. Other industries such as petroleum products and coal, chemicals, motor vehicles, tobacco, and paper were found to be relatively capital intensive.[4]

Fuchs has measured labor intensity in manufacturing by the ratio of wages paid production workers to value added by manufacture.[5] He found the average ratio for all manufacturing in 1954 to be 38.1 per cent. Among the twelve industry groups with averages above this level (relatively labor intensive) were: textiles; apparel; lumber; furniture; leather; stone, clay and glass; and miscellaneous manufacturing. In these industries the average wage per produc-

3. M. L. Greenhut and M. R. Colberg, *Factors in the Location of Florida Industry* (Tallahassee: Florida State University Studies No. 36, 1962), p. 70.

4. Perloff, *op. cit.*, p. 572.

5. Fuchs, *op. cit.*, p. 167.

tion worker was relatively low. However, high ratios of wages to value added were also found in the following high-wage industries: rubber, primary metals, fabricated metals, machinery, and transportation equipment.

The analysis presented by Fuchs covers all of the census regions in the United States. So far as the South is concerned, comparative gains in manufacturing employment between 1929 and 1954 were registered for all three divisions in each category (low wages and labor intensive, low wages and non-labor intensive, high wages and labor intensive, and high wages and non-labor intensive) except for the South Atlantic division in the high wages and non-labor intensive category. The South Atlantic and East South Central divisions made their largest gains in the low-wage industries but the gains were somewhat larger in non-labor intensive industries (food, tobacco, pulp and paper). These tend to be material-oriented industries, so the combination of material availability and lower wages apparently constituted the main stimulus to southern manufacturing progress. The West South Central States made their largest relative employment gain in the high wages and labor intensive industries. These consist of the rubber, primary metals, fabricated metals, machinery and transportation equipment industries.

Fuchs' book also contains excellent (four-digit) industry detail based on special availability of census data. He was able to show, for example, that the West South Central region made its largest comparative gain in employment in organic and inorganic chemicals and aircraft and parts. Largest gains were made in the East South Central division in shirts and nightwear and men's and boys' coats and suits. The South Atlantic states had the largest gains in cotton goods and synthetic textiles.

In line with the emphasis on human capital in the present study it appears desirable to break down the payroll in manufacturing as shown in the Census of Manufactures in such a way as to separate the contribution of professional workers from that of other labor. Any such separation must be a rough one, but the alternative of treating the services of both chemists and charwomen as labor is more likely to

TABLE 6-1.   GROWTH OF SOUTHERN MANUFACTURING, 1939-1959

Industry*	Value Added by Manufacturing ($ million)	
	1939	1958
Chemicals and allied products	419.0	4,242.0
Food and kindred products	582.2	3,812.3
Textiles	652.4	2,793.3
Primary metals	276.3	2,015.2
Transportation equipment	102.2	1,968.7
Paper and allied products	138.1	1,487.7
Stone, clay and glass products	154.7	1,283.0
Tobacco products	245.0	1,257.4
Fabricated metal products	129.1	1,221.2
Apparel	145.9	1,218.0
Printing	206.0	1,129.3
Machinery (except electrical)	94.6	1,100.5
Electrical machinery	23.3	1,090.1
Petroleum products	188.2	1,051.1
Lumber products, except furniture	270.0	913.0
Furniture and fixtures	85.6	686.8
Rubber and plastics products	4.7	438.7
Miscellaneous manufacturing	31.2	438.5
Leather products	36.0	205.8
Instruments and related products	1.4	138.3
Total	3,785.9	28,490.9

* Ranked according to size in 1958.
Source: *Census of Manufactures,* 1947 (for 1939 data) and 1958.

be misleading. It would be desirable also to separate the contribution of skilled workers from that of ordinary workers, but this does not appear to be feasible. While the contribution of professional persons to value added does not constitute the entire contribution of human capital to production, this calculation should be indicative in a preliminary way of the industries which are relatively "human capital intensive."

GROWTH INDUSTRIES IN THE SOUTH

Before calculating the importance of professional persons in manufacturing, it is interesting to note which

77

TABLE 6-2. SOUTHERN MANUFACTURING IN RELATION TO
ENTIRE NATION

Industry	Value Added as Per Cent of National Total		Absolute Change in Percentage of National Total (%)
	1939	1958	1939 to 1958
Textiles	35.8	57.5	+21.7
Tobacco products	70.0	88.9	+18.9
Petroleum products	27.0	41.7	+14.7
Rubber and plastic products	1.1	13.3	+12.2
Chemicals and allied products	23.0	34.5	+11.5
Paper and allied products	15.5	26.0	+10.5
Apparel	10.5	20.2	+ 9.7
Furniture and fixtures	20.4	29.2	+ 8.8
Electrical machinery	2.4	10.4	+ 8.0
Transportation equipment	5.7	12.8	+ 7.1
Stone, clay and glass products	18.0	23.2	+ 5.2
Food and kindred products	16.7	21.7	+ 5.0
Leather products	6.1	10.8	+ 4.7
Primary metals	12.7	17.2	+ 4.5
Instruments and related products	0.4	4.7	+ 4.3
Miscellaneous manufacturing	4.9	9.2	+ 4.3
Machinery (except electrical)	4.6	8.8	+ 4.2
Fabricated metal products	9.2	12.9	+ 3.7
Printing	11.6	14.2	+ 2.6
Lumber and products, except furniture	36.9	28.7	— 8.2
Total	15.7	20.1	+ 4.4

Source: *Census of Manufactures,* 1947 (for 1939 data) and 1958.

(two-digit) industries are largest in the South, and especially to measure gains relative to the nation as a whole. Table 6-1 shows value added by manufacture in 1939 and 1958, with industries listed according to their 1958 size. In both years chemicals, food products, textiles, and primary metals led the list, but the chemical industry replaced the textile industry in the top spot. Food products also moved ahead of textiles over the nineteen-year period.

The southern textile industry, nevertheless, made the best showing as measured in Table 6-2. Here the value added in the southern states is expressed as a percentage of value added in the same industry for the whole United States. The absolute gain in the southern share of value added in each industry is shown in the third column. In this relative sense the South made its greatest gains in textiles, tobacco products, petroleum products, rubber and plastic products, chemicals, paper, and apparel. The only (two-digit) industry classification in which the South suffered a relative loss was in lumber products (except furniture).

It should be kept in mind that the South would show declines in some lines of manufacturing even within the faster growing two-digit industries. Also, some of the southern states would show declines relative to the country as a whole even where the region has gained. The reader is referred to Fuchs' *Changes in the Location of Manufacturing in the U.S.* for this detail for the period 1929-54. For example, he shows a relative loss in manufacturing employment in logging, sawmills, and millwork in both the West South Central and East South Central regions, and also a fairly sharp loss in relative employment in motor vehicles and equipment in the latter. Such four-digit industries as fertilizers, gum and wood chemicals, men's and boys' furnishings, and tin cans had comparative employment losses in the South Atlantic states.[6] Comparative employment gains shown by Fuchs for the South are usually much larger than the losses. Especially large comparative employment gains were shown in the Southeast for cotton goods, synthetic textiles, and hosiery; in the East South Central states for shirts and nightwear, men's and boys' coats and suits, and inorganic and organic chemicals; and in the West South Central section for inorganic and organic chemicals, aircraft and parts (except engines), and machinery and other metal products.

GROWTH INDUSTRIES BY STATE

The same type of information as shown for the South as a whole in Table 6-2 is shown for southern states

6. Fuchs, *op. cit.*, p. 206.

TABLE 6-3. PRINCIPAL GROWTH INDUSTRIES IN SOUTHERN STATES, 1939-58, RELATIVE TO THE ENTIRE UNITED STATES

State	Industry	Value Added by Manufacture, 1958 As Per Cent of U.S. Total for Industry		
		1939 (%)	1958 (%)	Gain in Per Cent of U.S. (%)
Alabama	Apparel	0.2	1.4	1.2
	Paper	0.8	1.9	1.1
	Textiles	2.6	3.6	1.0
	Stone, clay, glass	0.9	1.5	0.6
	Primary metals	3.5	4.0	0.5
Arkansas	Leather	a	1.0	1.0
	Paper	0.4	1.1	0.7
	Furniture	0.8	1.3	0.5
	Apparel	*	0.4	0.4
	Chemicals	0.2	0.4	0.2
Delaware	Rubber and plastics	b	0.4	0.4
	Apparel	0.1	0.4	0.3
	Chemicals	0.6	0.7	0.1
	Fabricated metals	0.1	0.2	0.1
	Primary metals	0.1	0.2	0.1
Florida	Stone, clay, glass	0.4	1.9	1.5
	Chemicals	0.5	1.9	1.4
	Paper	1.2	2.6	1.4
	Furniture	0.4	1.6	1.2
	Fabricated metals	0.1	1.1	1.0
Georgia	Textiles	5.4	9.1	3.7
	Paper	1.4	4.0	2.6
	Transportation equipment	c	1.6	1.6
	Apparel	1.6	2.9	1.3
	Food	1.3	1.9	0.6
Kentucky	Tobacco	6.6	16.6	10.0
	Electrical machinery	0.5	2.2	1.7
	Chemicals	0.4	1.6	1.2
	Machinery, except electrical	0.4	1.0	0.6
	Apparel	0.5	1.1	0.6
Louisiana	Petroleum	2.3	8.0	5.7
	Chemicals	1.6	2.5	0.9
	Primary metals	*	0.7	0.7
	Stone, clay, glass	0.6	1.2	0.6
	Paper	2.7	3.2	0.5
Maryland	Rubber and Plastics	1.1	2.2	1.1
	Paper	0.9	1.3	0.4
	Primary metals	3.3	3.6	0.3
	Furniture	0.9	1.2	0.3
	Stone, clay, glass	1.5	1.7	0.2
Mississippi	Furniture	*	1.2	1.2
	Paper	0.6	1.4	0.8
	Apparel	0.5	1.2	0.7

TABLE 6-3 (CONT.)

State	Industry	Value Added by Manufacture, 1958 As Per Cent of U.S. Total for Industry		
		1939 (%)	1958 (%)	Gain in Per Cent of U.S. (%)
	Transportation equipment	b	0.4	0.4
	Stone, clay, glass	0.3	0.6	0.3
North Carolina	Tobacco products	34.4	47.0d	12.6
	Textiles	14.5	20.8	6.3
	Furniture	6.7	8.9	2.2
	Apparel	0.5	1.9	1.4
	Electrical machinery	b	1.3	1.3
Oklahoma	Petroleum	2.6	4.3	1.7
	Transportation equipment	*	0.4	0.4
	Stone, clay, glass	0.8	1.2	0.4
	Fabricated metals	0.4	0.7	0.3
	Machinery, except electrical	0.4	0.6	0.2
South Carolina	Textiles	6.1	13.6	7.5
	Chemicals	0.2	1.8	1.6
	Apparel	0.1	1.4	1.3
	Paper	0.9	1.4	0.5
	Stone, clay, glass	0.4	0.8	0.4
Tennessee	Leather	1.4	3.7	2.3
	Rubber and plastics	b	2.0	2.0
	Electrical machinery	*	1.1	1.1
	Textiles	2.2	3.2	1.0
	Paper	0.9	1.9	1.0
	Apparel	1.3	2.2	0.9
Texas	Chemicals	1.5	8.5	7.0
	Petroleum	17.6	23.5	5.9
	Transportation equipment	0.6	3.9	3.3
	Primary metals	0.2	2.5	2.3
	Stone, clay, glass	2.2	4.2	2.0
Virginia	Textiles	2.3	4.2	1.9
	Furniture	3.6	4.4	0.8
	Electrical machinery	b	0.6	0.6
	Apparel	0.8	1.2	0.4
	Food	0.9	1.3	0.4
West Virginia	Chemicals	2.5	3.2	0.7
	Primary metals	2.2	2.7	0.5
	Electrical machinery	0.2	0.5	0.3
	Machinery, except electrical	0.1	0.2	0.1

Source of original data: U.S. *Census of Manufactures,* 1947 (for 1939) and 1958.
  * Less than 0.1 per cent of U.S.
  a Not listed. Assumed to be negligible in 1939.
  b Not listed separately. Believed to be less than 0.1 per cent of U. S.
  c Not listed separately. Automobile industry was small in 1939.
  d Partly estimated; exact total is not disclosed by Bureau of Census.

in Table 6-3. For each state the five industries which grew most relative to the country as a whole between the 1939 and 1958 manufacturing censuses are listed.[7] Industries such as textiles, apparel, and chemicals which are near the top for the South as a whole in Table 6-2 are prominent in Table 6-3 also. The lumber and wood products industry, which declined relatively in the South, does not appear on the "rapid growth" list for any southern state. The same is true for the printing and publishing industry which gained only a little in the South relative to the United States as a whole. The furniture industry, however, appears as a large gainer, relative to the country, in five southern states.

ESTIMATING THE CONTRIBUTION OF PROFESSIONALS

The U.S. Census of Manufactures shows only the payroll related to "production workers" as a component of the total payroll in manufacturing. It appears to be feasible, however, to estimate the total pay to professionals in each industry in 1958 by making use of the 1960 *Census of Population*. Since information on income from the latter source pertains to 1959—only one year later than the Census of Manufactures—the joint use of the two censuses is probably less risky than it would appear to be.[8]

For most of the two-digit industries the number of professional persons employed within each state can be secured from Table 125 of the Detailed Characteristics volume for the same state. Median earnings for each profession can be obtained from Table 124 of the same reports. By assuming equal earnings for persons in a given profession in a state regardless of which industry they worked for, one can estimate the professional payroll for each industry in 1959. (The calculations were made separately for males and females.) Total payroll (professional and non-professional) for each industry can be estimated in a similar way from the Census of Population. This permits an estimate of the

7. Six industries are listed for Tennessee because the sixth grew almost as much as the fifth. Four are listed for West Virginia because no other two-digit industry grew significantly in relation to the United States total.

8. See Table V (Appendix) for a sample computation of the per cent of value added by manufacture attributable to professional persons.

TABLE 6-4. ESTIMATED PROPORTION OF VALUE ADDED BY EACH FACTOR, 1958, FOR PRINCIPAL GROWTH INDUSTRIES IN SOUTHERN STATES

State	Industry	Per cent of Value Added by		
		Skilled and Unskilled Labor	Professional Workers	Material Capital
Alabama	Apparel	53.2	2.9	43.9
	Paper	39.3	6.0	54.1
	Textiles	59.1	3.1	37.8
	Stone, clay, glass	32.7	6.5	60.8
	Primary metals	41.6	4.9	53.5
Arkansas	Leather	40.1	4.3	55.6
	Paper	37.2	4.0	58.8
	Furniture	61.1	5.1	33.8
	Apparel	65.3	3.3	31.4
	Chemicals	30.1	6.5	63.4
Delaware	Rubber and plastics	51.9	13.2	34.9
	Apparel	28.2	11.6	60.2
	Chemicals	17.5	18.8	63.7
	Fabricated metals	47.0	10.6	42.4
	Primary metals	55.4	20.4	24.2
Florida	Stone, clay, glass	34.0	10.3	55.7
	Chemicals	21.0	7.1	71.8
	Paper	37.2	5.2	57.6
	Furniture	52.8	7.6	39.6
	Fabricated metals	36.9	18.8	44.3
Georgia	Textiles	58.2	4.2	37.6
	Paper	30.6	4.6	64.8
	Transportation equipment	43.7	13.2	43.1
	Apparel	54.4	3.4	42.2
	Food	31.1	8.7	60.2
Kentucky	Tobacco	15.5	2.3	82.2
	Electrical machinery	29.8	5.2	65.0
	Chemicals	20.9	8.2	70.9
	Machinery, except electrical	39.3	9.9	50.8
	Apparel	61.1	3.1	35.8
Louisiana	Petroleum	28.9	7.8	53.3
	Chemicals	24.8	6.3	68.9
	Primary metals	23.3	3.1	73.6
	Stone, clay, glass	35.3	6.8	57.9
	Paper	38.2	7.7	54.1
Maryland	Rubber and plastics	44.6	6.2	49.2
	Paper	49.4	9.5	41.1
	Primary metals	44.7	4.0	51.3
	Furniture	48.7	9.7	41.6
	Stone, clay, glass	34.6	9.1	56.3

TABLE 6-4 (Cont.)

State	Industry	Per cent of Value Added by		
		Skilled and Unskilled Labor	Professional Workers	Material Capital
Mississippi	Furniture	50.2	4.6	45.2
	Paper	42.8	5.3	51.9
	Apparel	66.8	3.3	29.9
	Transportation equipment	79.2	8.3	12.5
	Stone, clay, glass	33.7	5.5	60.8
North Carolina	Tobacco products	13.9	2.5	83.6
	Textiles	56.2	4.0	39.8
	Furniture	53.6	4.8	41.6
	Apparel	57.1	3.4	39.5
	Electrical machinery	30.3	11.3	58.4
Oklahoma	Petroleum	23.8	9.9	66.3
	Transportation equipment	67.5	14.3	18.2
	Stone, clay, glass	36.7	6.5	56.8
	Fabricated metals	43.8	11.5	44.7
	Machinery, except electrical	46.9	12.8	40.3
South Carolina	Textiles	56.9	3.3	39.8
	Chemicals	28.5	7.0	64.5
	Apparel	61.5	3.4	35.1
	Paper	36.3	5.8	57.9
	Stone, clay, glass	37.4	5.6	57.0
Tennessee	Leather	39.0	6.3	54.7
	Rubber and plastics	32.5	4.1	63.4
	Electrical machinery	32.5	5.7	61.8
	Textiles	51.6	4.5	43.9
	Paper	34.2	5.4	60.4
	Apparel	59.7	2.8	37.5
Texas	Chemicals	17.9	5.1	77.0
	Petroleum	37.6	8.9	53.5
	Transportation equipment	42.5	19.3	38.2
	Primary metals	38.8	4.9	56.3
	Stone, clay, glass	28.8	7.4	63.8
Virginia	Textiles	50.4	4.0	45.6
	Furniture	48.8	4.8	46.4
	Electrical machinery	21.7	18.3	60.0
	Apparel	63.9	4.9	31.2
	Food	35.7	7.6	56.7
West Virginia	Chemicals	28.3	7.7	64.0
	Primary metals	38.9	4.3	56.8
	Electrical machinery	28.2	3.8	68.0
	Machinery, except electrical	54.0	12.1	33.9

Source: Estimated by author from data in 1958 *Census of Manufactures* and *U.S. Census of Population: 1960, Detailed Characteristics*, Final Report PC(1)2D-52D, Tables 124 and 125.

proportion of the payroll devoted to professional salaries. It was assumed that the same proportion of the 1958 payroll, by industry and state, was accounted for by professional workers.[9]

The contribution of material capital to value added by manufacture (which was called quasi-rent in Chapter 3) can be calculated by deducting total payroll from value added by manufacture. Since payroll can be broken down (roughly) into its professional and non-professional components in the manner indicated above, it is possible to prepare a tabulation of the percentage contribution of skilled and unskilled labor, professional workers, and material capital, to value added by manufacture in 1958. Table 6-4 shows this breakdown for each southern state for the principal growth industries of each state.

For any given industry shown in Table 6-4 there is a good deal of similarity from state to state in the percentage of value contributed by professional persons. Delaware is out of line with the other states, however, due perhaps to the importance of research and development activities at the duPont facilities. The importance of professionals in the value-added data is much higher in Delaware than in other states for rubber and plastic products, apparel, chemicals, and primary metals.

The estimated average contribution of professional persons to value added by manufacture in the South in 1958 is shown in Table 6-5. The table covers only industries shown in the earlier tables. At the bottom of the scale in professional labor intensiveness (and probably in human capital intensiveness) are tobacco products (2.4 per cent), textiles (3.8 per cent), apparel (4.2 per cent) and leather products (5.3 per cent). In each case there is a good deal

9. Several sources of error are involved in the process. A large new plant could change an industry substantially in one year within a given state. There are some differences in the classification of smaller industries in the two censuses; inter-industry differences within a state in the pay of a given type of professional worker cannot be taken into account; and median earnings are used whereas mean salaries would be appropriate. A value judgment as to whether the resulting estimates are close enough to be useful is involved. Pending better collection of data the present writer (obviously) considers the estimates to be worthwhile.

of consistency in the percentage contribution of professionals from state to state, except for apparel in Delaware.

At the top of the scale in the importance of the professional contribution to value added by manufacture are machinery (non-electrical), transportation equipment, and fabricated metal products. There tends to be greater variation from state to state for these products, probably because of the greater heterogeneity of products within these industry classifications. Transportation equipment, for example, includes aircraft, which uses many professionally trained persons, and trailer manufacture, where ordinary labor contributes most of the value to the manufacturing process. It may be noted that in Texas, where the aircraft industry has made great progress, almost one-fifth of the value added in the transportation equipment field was accounted for by professional persons, according to these rough estimates. On the other hand, it is probable that trailer manufacturing is largely responsible for the relatively low professional component in Mississippi's transportation equipment industry.

Inspection of Table 6-4 reveals little relationship between the professional contribution and the material capital contribution. (The rank correlation is close to zero.) The tobacco industry, for example, is material capital intensive but uses relatively few professional persons. The non-electrical machinery industry does not rank high in material capital intensiveness but ranks highest in the professional contribution to value added. In general, it appears that standardization or lack of standardization of the product is the most important determinant of the use of professional persons in manufacture. Relatively standardized products are usually found in the tobacco products, textile, apparel, leather, and paper industries, which rank low in use of professional persons. At the other end of the scale the machinery industry, transportation equipment, and fabricated metal products industry turn out more heterogeneous products, often on a made-to-order basis, and utilize relatively many professionals. The petroleum and chemical industries rank quite high in use of professional persons.

In part this is probably due to lack of separation in the census of research and development data from data on manufacturing.

While the coverage of industries in Table 6-3 is not sufficiently complete to permit a comprehensive listing of labor intensive and capital intensive industries, the estimated importance of professional workers is relevant to any such attempt. If the value contribution of professionals is considered to be a contribution of capital rather than of labor, it is doubtful that machinery production (both electrical and other), transportation equipment (other than trailers), and fabricated metal products manufacturing should be classified as labor intensive. This has sometimes been done, as was indicated earlier.

NON-WHITE PROFESSIONAL MEN IN SOUTHERN MANUFACTURING

Casual observation suggests that the growth of southern manufacturing in recent decades has not been accompanied by a substantial increase in professional positions for non-white men. If this is so it is probably traceable primarily to a relative lack of qualification for engineering, managerial, and other professional positions in manufacturing, and secondarily to discrimination in employment. The secondary factor can, of course, affect the primary factor through molding educational patterns. On the other hand, southern manufacturing growth has probably been an important stimulus to employment of white professional men in the region.

One way to test the above hypothesis is to compare the change in each southern state's percentage of the nation's stock of male college graduates from 1939 to 1959 with the change in the percentage contributed by that state to the national value added in manufacturing by professional persons. That is, one would expect such states as Texas, which sharply increased its share of the nation's value added in such fields as aircraft production, also to show a marked gain in its share of all white college graduates. On the other hand, West Virginia, which suffered a decline in its share of

TABLE 6-5. AVERAGE CONTRIBUTION OF PROFESSIONAL PERSONS
TO VALUE ADDED BY MANUFACTURE IN THE SOUTH, 1958

Industry	Percentage of Value Added by Professionals*
Machinery, except electrical	17.4
Transportation equipment	13.8
Fabricated metal products	13.6
Petroleum products	8.9
Electrical machinery	8.7
Chemicals and allied products	8.3
Food products	8.1
Rubber and plastic products	7.8
Stone, clay, and glass products	7.2
Primary metals	6.9
Furniture and fixtures	6.1
Paper and allied products	5.9
Leather products	5.3
Apparel	4.2
Textiles	3.8
Tobacco products	2.4

* Unweighted averages derived from column 2, Table 6-5.

the nation's value added by manufacturing between 1939 and 1958, would be expected also to have a reduced share of white male college-educated men in its population. The decline in the latter would be expected to be related also to the kind of manufacturing that declined relatively in West Virginia. For example, the relative decline in the textile industry, which does not use many professional men would not carry a great deal of weight in determining whether college-educated persons would leave West Virginia.

As a consequence of this need to consider the *kind* of industry that changed in importance, the 1939-1958 change in each state's percentage of the national value added, by industry, was weighted by the percentage of value added by professional persons (derived as described previously). More specifically, the gain in per cent of U.S. value added, as shown in the right-hand column of Table 6-3 was weighted by the per cent of value added by professional labor as shown in the second data column in Table 6-4.

TABLE 6-6. RANKINGS OF SOUTHERN STATES IN SPECIFIED
CHANGES OVER TWO DECADES

State	Change in Wtd. Average Share of U.S. Value Added 1939-1958	Change in Share of U.S. College-educated White Males, 25 and Over 1939-1959	Change in Share of U.S. College-educated Non-White Males, 25 and Over 1939-1959
Texas	1	1	14
North Carolina	2	8	16
Florida	3	2	1
South Carolina	4	11	7
Georgia	5	5	12
Louisiana	6	6	4
Kentucky	7	14	10
Tennessee	8	9	11
Alabama	9	7	3
Mississippi	10	13	6
Oklahoma	11	15	15
Arkansas	12	12	13
Virginia	13	3	8
Delaware	14	10	5
Maryland	15	4	2
West Virginia	16	16	9

Sources of data: U.S. *Census of Manufactures,* 1939 and 1958, *and* U.S. *Census of Population,* 1940 and 1960, with estimates and computations as indicated in text.

Since the industries covered in these tables are only the principal growth industries, it was necessary also to consider the other two-digit industries in each state. For these additional industries, the per cent of value added by professionals was not estimated specifically for the state but was entered on the basis of the average in other states for the same industry.

It is recognized that the resulting data are subject to substantial errors in addition to those involved in the computations presented in Table 6-4. Nevertheless, they appear to be adequate for a rough test of the broad hypothesis that white male college graduates have been attracted to the South (or induced to stay in the South) by the relative growth of manufacturing in the region while this growth has had little or no tendency to attract or retain non-white male college graduates.

In Table 6-6 (Col. 1), the sixteen southern states are ranked according to the growth from 1939 to 1958 in their share of the total U.S. value added by manufacturing, weighted by value added by professionals. In Column 2 a ranking of the change in percentage of the nation's white male college graduates (25 years and over) is given, while Column 3 shows a similar ranking for non-white males with four or more years of college education. Texas, which increased its share of all white male college graduates in the country by the greatest amount (from 3.9 to 5.1 per cent) between the 1940 and 1960 censuses, is shown to rank first in the first two columns. West Virginia, where the share of the nation's white male college graduates declined from 0.9 per cent in 1939 to 0.6 per cent in 1959 ranks lowest in both columns. Florida ranks first in Column 3 since its share of the non-white male college educated population rose most between these census years—from 2.3 to 2.8 per cent of the nation's total. (Florida is the only southern state in which this percentage increased.) North Carolina ranks sixteenth in Column 3 since its percentage of the non-white males with sixteen or more years of education declined most—from 5.8 to 3.9 per cent. (It should be noted that these rankings are in terms of the *change* over the twenty-year period. Texas and North Carolina in 1959 had the largest actual shares of well-educated non-white men among the southern states.)

From the rankings shown in Table 6-6 a Spearman rank correlation of +0.41 is obtained between Columns 1 and 2 and of −0.24 between Columns 1 and 3. Both of these rank correlations would have been higher were it not for the strong attraction of increased federal employment in Washington, D.C., to both white and non-white college graduates. This employment has greatly increased the college-educated white population in the "dormitory states" of Virginia and Maryland, and has had a substantial effect on the well educated population of these states. If these two states are omitted, the rank correlation becomes +0.72 (significant at .01) for white males and −0.14 for non-white males. The results of this test suggest that the relative growth of southern manufacturing during the two decades under examination was important in attracting or keeping white males with college degrees. However, the southern states that gained most in appropriate types of manufacturing activity during the two decades did not hold or attract non-white male college students to a greater degree than did other southern states. Broadly speaking, the investigations described in the present and previous chapters suggest strongly that segregated education has been a powerful force in providing employment in the South for college-educated Negro women and in stimulating these women to secure university degrees but that the relative growth of manufacturing in the region did not have similar effects on Negro males.

Our glorious land to-day,
'Neath education's sway,
Soars upwards still.
Its halls of learning fair,
Whose bounties all may share,
Behold them everywhere,
On vale and hill.

> —Samuel Francis Smith,
> "America" (discarded stanza)

CHAPTER VII
INCOME AND EDUCATION:
SOUTH AND NON-SOUTH

RECENT YEARS have witnessed an increasing recognition among economists, government officials, and others of the close relationship between unemployment and inadequate education. In part this is traceable to the greater ease of substituting machines for men in many types of routine jobs which are not highly demanding mentally. There have been numerous articles and books dealing with the plight of the school drop-out, for example.

Similarly, the gains in income attributable to education —especially above the secondary school level—have been attracting increasing attention. The examination of this matter may take the form of estimating stocks of human capital built into individuals by means of education, or, more simply, in terms of reported annual earnings. The former approach will be used in the next chapter; the simpler one in the present chapter.

When gains in earnings for any given sex, age, and race category are attributed to differences in education, the analyst is apt to assume that other things are equal. However, such attributes as good physical and mental endowment and health, ambition, interest from material capital owned, and urban residence are positively correlated with educational attainment. As a consequence, the gains attributable to formal education are likely to be overstated. Nevertheless, census data collected for a sample of the population in 1940, 1950, and 1960 show so marked an increase in yearly income as more schooling is completed that there is little doubt of the high importance of this variable, *ceteris paribus*.

INCOME IN RELATION TO EDUCATION, RACE, SEX, AND REGION

Most users of these census data have devoted principal attention to the income of males.[1] The present and next chapters will pay equal attention to incomes and capital values of females. Data from the 1960 census, which have only recently (late 1963) become available, will be utilized along with similar data from the 1950 and 1940 censuses in order to discover trends in the relation between income and education.

Tables 7-1, 7-2, 7-3, and 7-4 show data for 1939, 1949, and 1959 relating median income and education, by age group of recipient, separately for the South and non-South. Table 7-1 pertains to white males, 7-2 to non-white males, 7-3 to white females, and 7-4 to non-white females. The income information in the 1940 census was limited to wages and salaries, while for the later censuses earnings from all sources are included. For lower-income persons the difference between all earnings and wage or salary income is undoubtedly small, but it probably increases with both age

1. Morton Zeman, in *op. cit.*, makes some remarks about income of females but limits most of his analysis to males due to the availability of better information. Herman P. Miller, *Income of the American People* (New York: Wiley, 1955), shows data for men 35 to 44, by years of school completed and race, by regions. Burton A. Weisbrod, "The Valuation of Human Capital," *Journal of Political Economy*, LXIX, October 1961, p. 425, utilizes earnings data for males only.

TABLE 7-1. MEDIAN INCOME BY AGE AND EDUCATION—WHITE MALES
(DOLLARS)

Age	8 Years		12 Years		16 or More Years	
	South	Non-South	South	Non-South	South	Non-South
			1939			
18-19	382	385	438	418	595	511
20-21	476	524	657	657	652	718
22-24	590	686	888	923	823	1018
25-29	756	906	1162	1218	1621	1633
30-34	941	1122	1487	1565	2214	2239
35-44	1144	1355	1833	1963	2712	2916
45-54	1269	1439	2004	2176	2063	3148
55-65	1177	1286	1911	2009	2767	2886
			1949			
18-19	826	978	722	790	—	—
20-21	1246	1488	1405	1741	961	803
22-24	1590	2033	2174	2383	1561	1512
25-29	2039	2412	2781	2962	2982	2947
30-34	2222	2723	3240	3374	4308	4262
35-44	2344	2964	3460	3585	5167	5209
45-54	2366	3050	3610	3757	5520	5637
55-64	2001	2746	3232	3468	5004	5242
			1959			
18-19	1017	1363	—	—	—	—
20-21	1766	2150	2055	2704	1449	1981
22-24	2378	3075	3108	3805	2596	2767
25-29	3202	4118	4354	5040	5148	5454
30-34	3841	4684	5160	5700	7149	7504
35-44	4034	4865	5570	6046	8730	9081
45-54	3817	4912	5566	5976	9094	9630
55-64	3268	4565	5082	5602	8162	9096

Source: *U.S. Census of Population*, 1940, Education, Educational Attainment by
Economic Characteristics and Martial Status, tables 29 through 38. *U.S. Census
of Population*, 1950, Special Report P.E. No. 58, Education, Tables 12 and 13.
U.S. Census of Population, 1960, PC(2)5B, Educational Attainment, table 6.
1949 data for white and non-white males were computed by Burton Weisbrod
and reported by W. Hochwald and M. Megee, "The Industrial Composition of
the South and Its Bearing Upon the Economic Development of the Region," a
paper prepared for the Second Annual Conference, Inter-university Committee
for Economic Research on the South, New Orleans, Feb. 23-24, 1962.

TABLE 7-2.   MEDIAN INCOME BY AGE AND EDUCATION—
NON-WHITE MALES
(DOLLARS)

Age	8 Years		12 Years		16 or More Years	
	South	Non-South	South	Non-South	South	Non-South
1939						
18-19	307	395	357	445	—	—
20-21	379	439	423	509	—	—
22-24	415	582	484	677	618	667
25-29	505	692	612	816	891	1101
30-34	557	815	697	940	1020	1337
35-44	608	884	747	1062	1219	1470
45-54	615	893	832	1199	1307	1439
55-64	649	863	810	1180	1159	1375
1949						
18-19	534	782	531	697	—	—
20-21	983	1219	1032	1410	—	—
22-24	1226	1771	1262	2041	—	—
25-29	1411	2033	1676	2327	1830	2120
30-34	1568	2213	1892	2524	2391	2841
35-44	1607	2285	1998	2579	2830	3275
45-54	1532	2329	1879	2532	2738	3309
55-64	1239	2174	1618	2298	2317	2941
1959						
18-19	728	927	—	—	—	—
20-21	1111	1751	1389	1918	—	—
22-24	1592	2324	1905	2594	1562	2396
25-29	2110	3015	2599	3713	3270	3925
30-34	2392	3351	2896	4225	4192	5347
35-44	2569	3790	3150	4645	4722	6044
45-54	2435	3839	2989	4403	4930	6103
55-64	2059	3363	2500	4072	4354	5425

Source: See Table 7-1.

and education.[2]   Original sources include income data for educational attainment groups other than 8, 12, and 16 or

2. Figures shown here will not in all cases be precisely the same as those shown in other articles or books because of the unfortunate census practice of presenting data for some categories (e.g., total males and non-white males), and leaving other categories (e.g., white males) to be laboriously estimated by users. Residuals cannot be found precisely when median, rather than mean, data are published.

TABLE 7-3. MEDIAN INCOME BY AGE AND EDUCATION—
WHITE FEMALES
(DOLLARS)

	8 Years		12 Years		16 or More Years	
Age	South	Non-South	South	Non-South	South	Non-South
			1939			
18-19	362	365	398	392	464	547
20-21	423	453	533	568	595	606
22-24	469	531	653	708	779	854
25-29	519	626	786	839	975	1163
30-34	574	688	918	990	1101	1436
35-44	602	727	1028	1102	1205	1732
45-54	595	707	1039	1139	1337	1923
55-64	565	625	990	1021	1297	2017
			1949			
18-19	484	747	761	812	—	—
20-21	637	1030	1323	1610	—	—
22-24	713	1111	1520	1737	1722	1743
25-29	774	1103	1500	1694	2020	2207
30-34	837	1217	1487	1634	2059	2304
35-44	880	1397	1587	1778	2330	2563
45-54	869	1273	1690	1850	2505	2771
55-64	711	1031	1345	1520	2375	2705
			1959			
18-19	—	—	—	—	—	—
20-21	829	1040	1818	2364	1460	1508
22-24	923	1109	2049	2377	2409	2655
25-29	1053	1416	2152	2240	3105	3435
30-34	1238	1691	2254	2216	3055	3124
35-44	1452	1897	2348	2403	3576	3726
45-54	1419	2040	2473	2706	4131	4720
55-64	977	1505	1974	2484	4078	4786

Source: See Table 7-1.

more years, but these are not shown since it is believed they fail to add much to any analysis that can be made.[3]

3. Presentation of an excessive number of undigestable figures, ratios, changes, combinations, etc., appears to be a hazard of the electronic computer age.

TABLE 7-4.   MEDIAN INCOME BY AGE AND EDUCATION—
NON-WHITE FEMALES
(DOLLARS)

Age	8 Years		12 Years		16 or More Years	
	South	Non-South	South	Non-South	South	Non-South
			1939			
18-19	256	316	282	322	500	—
20-21	271	351	288	356	448	750
22-24	277	416	316	464	573	707
25-29	295	465	354	515	729	896
30-34	305	503	402	608	826	1193
35-44	319	509	435	630	880	1345
45-54	344	500	516	662	904	1209
55-64	336	491	444	527	935	1000
			1949			
18-19	341	575	344	491	—	—
20-21	406	755	460	984	—	—
22-24	444	1042	585	1285	1524	1609
25-29	503	1075	714	1329	1736	2035
30-34	570	1145	853	1406	2040	2235
35-44	574	1145	874	1406	2259	2528
45-54	518	1031	871	1310	2266	2231
55-64	447	950	696	1164	2054	2250
			1959			
18-19	—	—	—	—	—	—
20-21	636	923	719	1225	—	3032
22-24	635	1002	832	1588	2038	2723
25-29	722	1148	972	1984	3141	3477
30-34	777	1316	1133	2194	3521	3875
35-44	848	1562	1275	2330	3854	4338
45-54	810	1391	1205	2126	3998	4417
55-64	730	1094	926	1720	3723	3799

Source: See Table 7-1.

NORTH-SOUTH DIFFERENTIAL

Numerous significant comparisons of median incomes can be made from these data, especially by means of some further calculations and graphic presentation.   Figure

97

4 shows southern median incomes as a percentage of non-southern median incomes, thus emphasizing the North-South differential. (This term is losing meaning, however, as the far West is becoming an increasingly important region.) Parity of incomes is represented by the 100 per cent line. Figure 4 pertains to the important 30-34 year age group and shows the 1959 data separately for white males, white females, non-white males, and non-white females with eight, twelve, or sixteen and more years of schooling.

The three bars to the left in Figure 4 illustrate the fact that southern incomes are relatively low for unskilled white male workers, but that the better educated white men— especially college graduates—now earn nearly as much in the South as outside the region. If an adjustment were made for degree of urban residence, the difference would be even smaller. If further adjustment were made for the slightly lower cost of living in the South, the real income of college-educated white men might even show up as slightly higher in the South, *ceteris paribus*. Unfortunately, cost of living differences between localities are especially difficult to measure. It is particularly a problem to keep constant the quality of living in such measurements. Even for a single region, variation in quality of commodities over time presents a very great problem, as in the cost-of-living index.

Figure 4 also shows that poorly-educated white women in the South are even more disadvantaged than are white men with only eight years of schooling. Probably competition from large numbers of poorly educated Negro women is an important factor here. A high school diploma, however, appears to open up earnings opportunities for southern white women in secretarial and other work to an extent sufficient to give them nearly as much income as the same group outside the region. (For the 30-34 year age group the southern median was slightly above that for the non-South, but this was not the case at other ages.) Opportunities in the South for college-educated white women appear to have been slightly poorer than in the non-South, but the deviation from parity (Figure 4) is small.

In the case of non-white persons, both male and female,

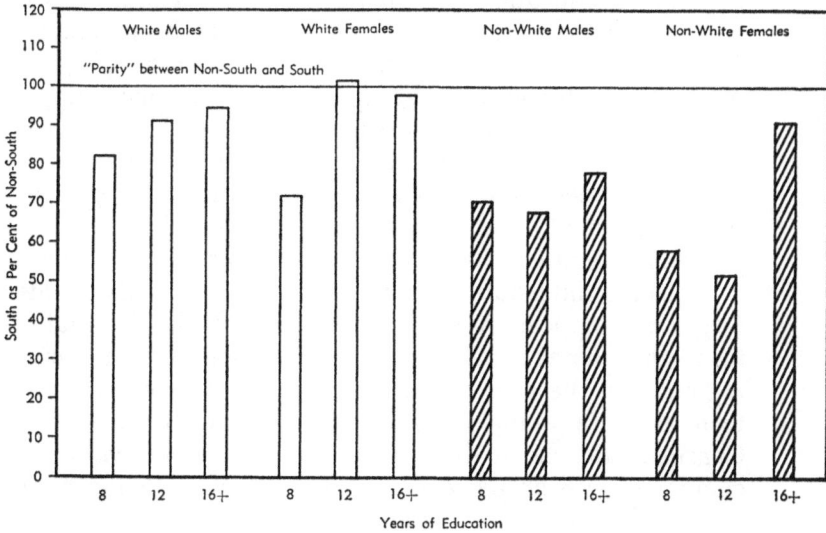

Figure 4 · Median Southern Incomes As Per Cent of Those Outside South
(Persons 30-34 Years of Age—1959)

a high school education does not appear to have helped earning power in the South relative to other regions, although absolute earnings are higher in the South for these high school graduates than for similar persons with grade school education. (See Tables 7-2 and 7-4.) College education, however, has greatly improved the earnings of southern Negro females relative to similarly situated non-southerners. Figure 4 indicates 91 per cent of parity for this group. As was discussed in some detail in Chapter V, the existence of largely segregated education in the South in 1959 along with the strong tendency of Negro female college graduates to be engaged in teaching, undoubtedly explains this situation. The positive correlation of urban residence and female teachers' salaries shown in Chapter 5 suggests that adjustment for urban-rural residence would show greater equality of southern and non-southern earnings for college educated non-white women.

College educated Negro males in the South show up better than the less-educated men in the non-white category in relation to earnings outside the region. Their gain

99

is not nearly so marked as that of Negro females, however. Segregated education has provided fewer teaching jobs for Negro men than for Negro women. It has been said that "teaching and preaching" provide most of the employment in the South for educated Negro men. Too many appear to have been occupied in preaching (where there is strong competition from less educated Negro men) compared with teaching (where competition from less-educated Negro men is not important) and where income is derived mainly from government rather than from impecunious private sources.

A lack of interstate mobility on the part of well-educated Negro men appears to be partly responsible for their failure to secure more equal monetary remuneration in various regions. In the case of the 30-34 year age group with sixteen or more years of education a recent Bureau of the Census report shows that 16 per cent of the non-white men compared with 26 per cent of the white men in the nation as a whole lived in a different state in 1955 and 1960.[4]

The relatively small numbers of Negro men who do hold college degrees in the South appear to have been handicapped by lack of technical education, by strong competition from Negro women for teaching jobs, by some lack of mobility, and by discrimination in employment in cases where qualifications are equal to those of white men.

OTHER INCOME COMPARISONS

Although the above discussion, geared to interregional comparisons, includes some of the same material, a clearer comparison of incomes for white and non-white males, and for white and non-white women can be obtained by holding region constant. Accordingly, Figures 5 and 6 pertain to the South and non-South, respectively, and show 1939 and 1959 median incomes for various age groups for white and non-white males separately. (Data for 1949 are not plotted since they tend to obscure the graphic picture.) It is clear that college educated non-white men are at a strong disadvantage in both the South and outside

4. U.S. *Census of Population: 1960 Subject Reports. Mobility for States and State Economic Areas,* Final Report PC (2)-2B, Table 6.

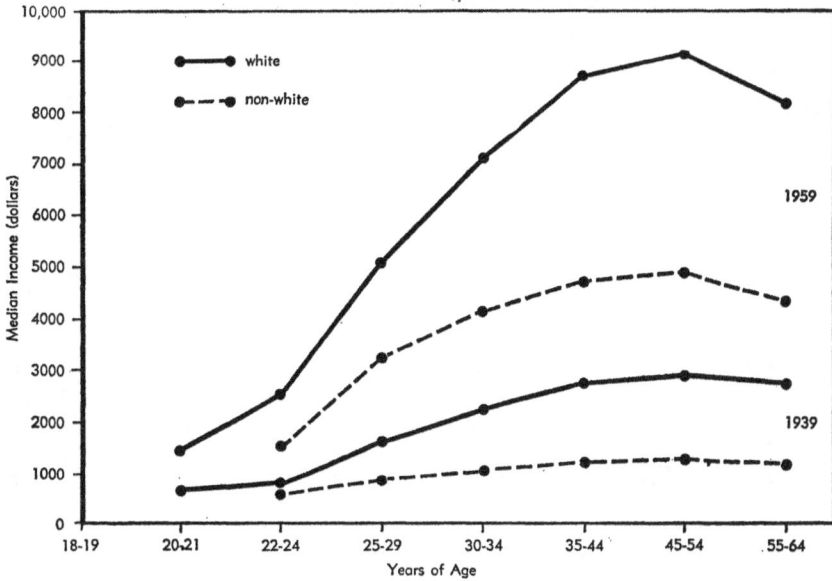

Figure 5 · Median Incomes, South
(Males with 16 or more years of education)

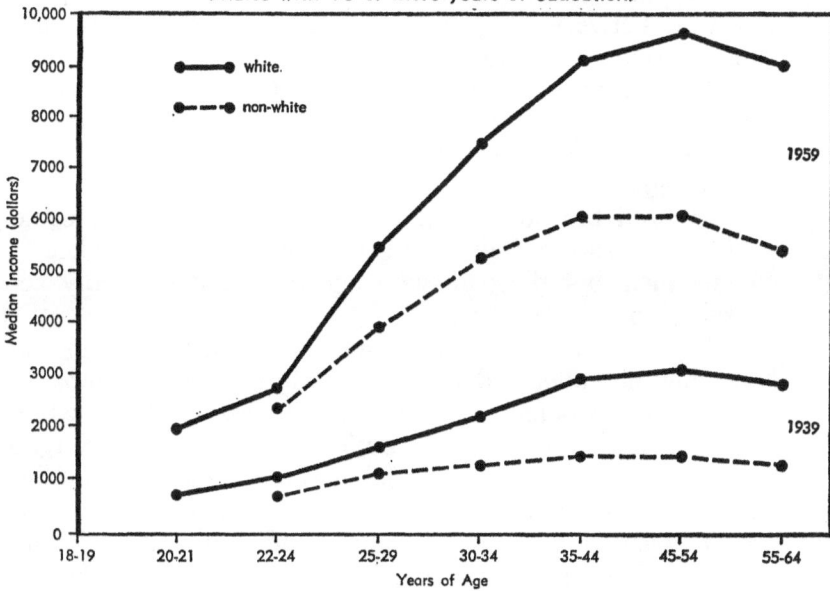

Figure 6 · Median Incomes, Non-South
(Males with 16 or more years of education)

Figure 7 · Median Incomes, South
(Females with 16 or more years of education)

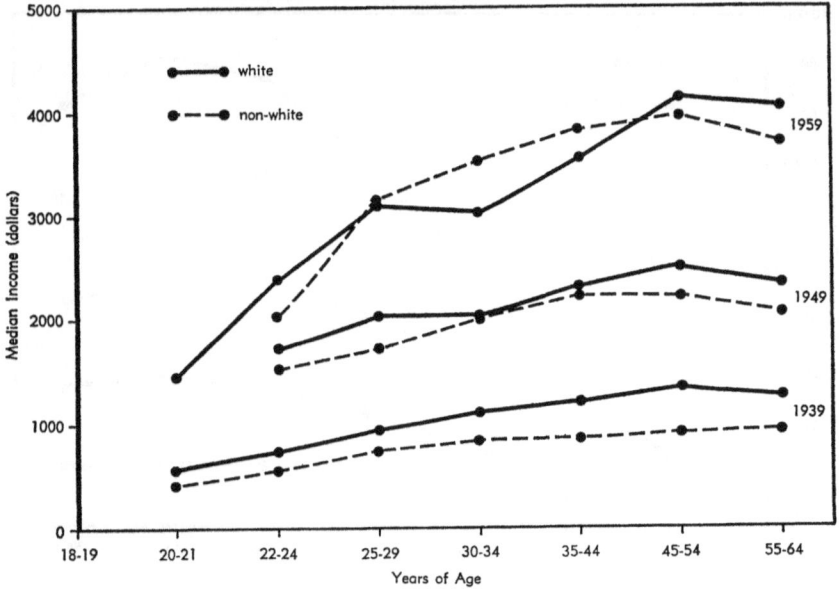

the region. Some improvement occurred in their relative position between 1939 and 1959, the gain being somewhat greater outside the South.

Income for well educated non-white males shows much less absolute improvement with age, although the peak is reached from 45 to 54 for non-whites as well as whites in both regions.

In both the South and non-South the gain in income with age was especially meager in 1939 for educated non-white men, but the gain with age improved markedly according to the 1959 data.

Figures 7 and 8 show a much different picture of the incomes of college-educated non-white women compared with white women. The advantage possessed by white women of all age groups in both regions in 1939 and 1949 was lost by 1959. Between the ages of 25 and 44 well educated non-white women had higher earnings than similar white women in both the South and non-South. White women above 44 years of age had better earnings, however.

This situation is similar to the apparent discrimination against white female school teachers mentioned in Chapter 5. The strong tendency of non-whites to live in the cities of the North largely explains why median incomes of educated non-white women are higher than those of comparably educated white women. In the South, however, this tendency is much less marked and, as has been stated previously, the relatively good income of educated non-white women in the South is probably attributable quite largely to segregated schooling. The high non-white birth rate, together with segregated schooling, has provided a strong and improving demand for non-white female school teachers. Also, the desire of many southern states to economize on education of non-white children has worked to the disadvantage of educated non-white men in the region in securing teaching employment.

A distinct tendency for median earnings to fall off more in the later years of life appears in the case of non-whites, both male and female, in all educational groups. This may

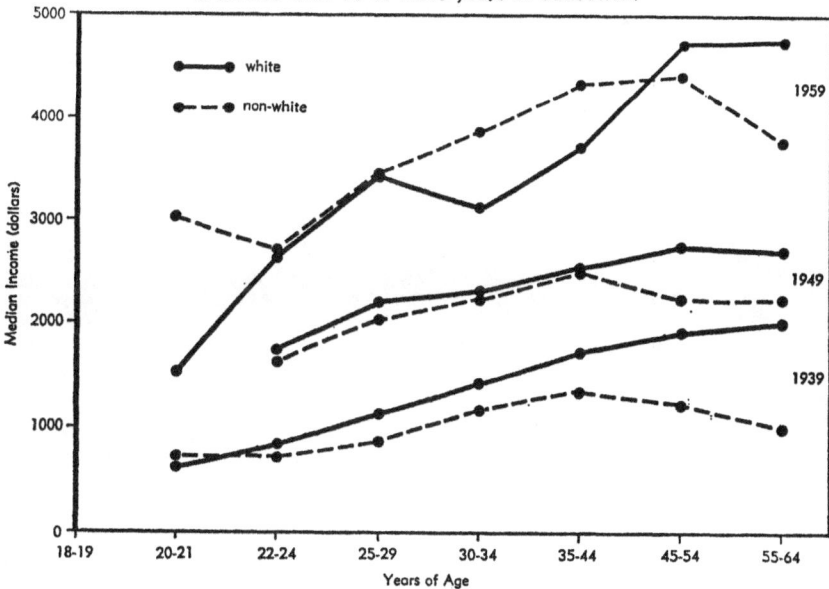

Figure 8 · Median Incomes, Non-South
(Females with 16 or more years of education)

be due in part to an earlier decline in health. Greater discrimination against older non-white persons is a further
possibility. Also, it is likely that rentier income of elderly
white persons is greater, and this income is included in the
data for 1949 and 1959.

Let early education be a sort of amusement; You will then be better able to find out the natural bent.

—Plato, *The Republic*

CHAPTER VIII
VALUE OF HUMAN CAPITAL
IN THE SOUTH AND NON-SOUTH

THE PREVIOUS CHAPTER emphasized earnings of persons in various categories (age, education, sex, and region of residence) at three census dates. These data, combined with census reports of the numbers of persons in each category, permit estimates of the value of human capital.

Shortcomings of the data available for the purpose at hand are numerous. Also, the absolute levels of human capital are greatly affected by estimates of the stage at which education begins to build capital into the individual, by the question "value to whom?," by the interest rate used to capitalize future earnings and by numerous other factors. Some of these were discussed in Chapter 2. As a consequence, the writer does not wish to imply that the present estimates are more accurate than other available estimates insofar as they pertain to the same categories. Rather, since the emphasis here is on the regional, racial, and sex breakdowns at various dates, more interest attaches to relative than to absolute magnitudes of human capital values.

Perhaps the inconsistency with other estimates should be reduced by denoting the present estimates as capital values of formal education beyond the elementary level rather than value of human capital. The simpler term is retained for convenience, however. In fact there appears to be much to be said for the definition of human capital used in the present study for purposes of regional analysis since the movement of relatively well-educated persons may be quite different from that of other persons.

The median income data shown in Tables 7-1 to 7-4 are taken from census reports (but involve a great deal of calculation and some arbitrary assumptions since some categories are not directly reported). For 1939, mean earnings from salaries and wages were reported, while in 1949 and 1959 median total income from all sources was reported. It was necessary to treat these medians as if they were arithmetic means of wage and salary income. It is at least comforting that very large incomes from material property do not affect median incomes greatly. That is, most of the income from non-human wealth is omitted, although the wage and salary income of better educated persons, especially older white persons, is somewhat overstated on this account.

For purposes of this study, 65 years was considered the upper age limit for wage and salary earners although obviously this is not entirely correct. The number of persons with income was used rather than the total number of persons in a given category. This raises the question whether the special capabilities of a well-educated housewife who is not a member of the active labor force constitutes part of the nation's stock of human capital. It appears better to omit her from this stock although she obviously might be very useful in a national emergency. Even under ordinary conditions she has an augmented value in such activities as supplementing the teaching received by her children.

A factor which keeps the absolute magnitude of human capital values shown in the present chapter far below some other estimates is the capitalization only of excess earnings above those obtained by a graduate of elementary school. This procedure is an alternative to that used by Burton Weisbrod,[1] who subtracts each earner's estimated personal consumption from his income. Weisbrod's idea seems similar to that of capitalizing the quasi-rent on a machine, i.e., of capitalizing income above variable costs of operating the machine. Personal consumption may be likened to a cost of operating the personal machine. However, a possible disadvantage of Weisbrod's method is that it does away with the labor factor, making all human quasi-rents a return to human capital. This can be defended philosophically, but there is such a sharp difference in the employment opportunities open to those with only an elementary education and those with further education that useful insights can be gained by the alternative procedure used in the present study. This is especially true when there is particular interest in regional movements. For example, it does not seem optimal to characterize the migration of poorly educated Negroes to the North as a capital movement. Under the procedure used in this study, only the movement of better educated Negroes and others shows up as a capital movement. A separation, admittedly arbitrary, is maintained between labor and human capital.

Deduction of earnings attributable to the first eight years of schooling sharply reduces the extra income to be capitalized. In the 30-34 year age group of males in 1950, for example, Weisbrod deducts personal consumption of $555 per year. For the same age group the present study deducts $2222 for southern white males, $2723 for non-southern white males, $1568 for southern non-white males, and $2213 for non-southern non-white males. It is primarily for this reason that the absolute magnitude of present estimates of human capital values are much lower than Weisbrod's. As already indicated, the present calculations are not estimates of the total value of education but only of the added value of high school and subsequent education. The excess incomes upon which capital values are based in the present chapter are shown in Table 8-1. Data are shown

1. "The Valuation of Human Capital," *Journal of Political Economy*, LXIX (Oct., 1961), 427.

only for the 35-44 age group but can be obtained readily for other groups from Tables 7-1, 7-2, 7-3, and 7-4. For example, the 1949 figure for white males in the non-South of age 30-34 attributes $1539 in yearly income to education beyond the eighth grade. This involves the further assumption that additional education is the only factor in the additional earning power of college graduates although this is obviously not wholly the case. At the same time it is evident from common observation that many persons who graduate from college would have done very poorly if they had remained in a low educational category and had been forced to be manual laborers.

TABLE 8-1. AVERAGE YEARLY EXCESS INCOME OF HIGH SCHOOL AND COLLEGE GRADUATES AGES 35 TO 44 YEARS

Region and Group	Excess Income for Persons with Twelve and Sixteen or More Years' Education: Data for 1939, 1949, 1959 (dollars)					
	1939		1949		1959	
	12	16+	12	16+	12	16+
South						
White males	689	1568	1116	2823	1536	4696
Non-white males	139	611	391	1223	581	2153
White females	426	603	707	1450	896	2124
Non-white females	116	561	300	1685	427	3006
Non-South						
White males	608	1561	621	2245	1181	4216
Non-white males	178	586	294	990	855	2254
White females	378	1005	381	1166	606	1829
Non-white females	121	836	261	1383	768	2776

Source: Tables 7-1, 7-2, 7-3, and 7-4. Median yearly income of persons with 12 and 16 or more years of schooling, minus median yearly income of persons in same race, sex, and regional category with 8 years of schooling.

Although many of the inferences that can be made from a comparison of such excess earnings are the same as those already made in Chapter 7 from inspection of actual median incomes, certain additional facts stand out. In general, the gains from education in the South show up as larger than before because of the greater disadvantage of ordinary laborers in the region compared with the non-South. These excess earnings are closely related to the incentive of persons within the South to continue their schooling beyond the eighth grade. They are not related, however, to the incentive of educated persons in the non-South to move, or not to move, to the South.

For white males, the excess earnings in the 35 to 44 year age group are consistently higher in the South than the non-South for all three census years and for both high school and college graduates. For the most part the same is true for white women in the South. For both groups the gain from escaping from the relatively untutored labor force into the groups which embody a good deal of immaterial capital is especially large.

For non-white males the dollar gains in income in this age group attributable to high school and higher degrees are generally lower than for whites in both the South and in the rest of the nation. Non-white females in the South do not benefit as much as do white women by securing high school diplomas. However, those who secure college degrees benefit to a greater extent since these are needed to enter the professions—especially teaching in segregated schools. In 1959, especially, the same advantage appears in the non-South for non-white women with college degrees, but such degrees are not quite so vital to earning power as in the South.

TOTAL EXCESS EARNINGS

Multiplication of excess earnings such as those shown in Table 8-1 by the number of persons with income in each of the age, sex, race, and regional categories gives total excess earnings for those with 12 years of schooling and 16 or more years of schooling. However, this leaves out the excess earnings of those who left high school or college before graduating. The most feasible way to calculate these earnings was to "blow up" the total excess earnings of the graduates by dividing by the per cent of total excess earnings for persons 25 years and older accounted for by those with 12 and 16+ years of formal education. Data for calculation of these percentages were reported separately by the Bureau of the Census for 1949 and 1959. (Percentages for 1949 were used by the author for 1939.) These percentages of excess earnings attributable to the 12 and 16+ groups were: white males 1949, 56 per cent; 1959, 58 per cent: white females, 1949, 59 per cent; 1959, 61 per cent: non-white males, 1949, 43 per cent; 1959, 46 per cent: non-white females, 1949, 48 per cent; 1959, 48 per cent. These percentages are of some interest in themselves, since they are related to a type of drop-out rate. Both white and non-white females have a somewhat better record from this point of view than males of the same race.

The aggregate excess earnings of persons with exactly 12 and with 16 or more years of schooling, are shown in Appendix Table VI, which also shows the number of such persons with income according to census reports (and the author's interpretations and assumptions).[2]

CAPITALIZATION OF EXCESS EARNINGS

Once estimated total excess earnings attributable to education beyond the eighth grade are on hand it is necessary to capitalize them. Probably the best procedure is that followed by Burton Weisbrod,[3] in which future excess income (as he defines it) for an individual in a given age bracket is adjusted to take into account the probability of his living through later age brackets. It was found that this procedure was unduly burdensome for the present study in view of the large number of categories related to sex, race, education, region, and census dates. Instead, total excess earnings calculated for each census date are capitalized as

2. Many assumptions have to be made by the analyst of earnings-education data. For example, persons who do not report years of education were treated as having none, although this is obviously not entirely correct. Net over-reporting of educational attainment is more common, however. The Bureau of the Census considered this to be especially true in 1950.

3. *Op. cit.*

if they were an income stream in perpetuity. This implicitly assumes that individuals with income will be replaced by others of equal attributes, so that the income stream is unaltered through time. A potential defect of the method is that it fails to take into account such variables as changes in age distribution between one census and the next. However, it has been emphasized that in the present study less interest attaches to absolute capital values than to relative values. These relative values should not be so strongly affected as are absolute values by the capitalization method used. Also, according to Roy L. Lassiter, Jr., the results of perpetuity calculation do not differ greatly from the more complex procedure followed by Weisbrod.[4]

The simplifying assumption of a uniform income stream in perpetuity requires only that aggregate excess income be divided by an appropriate interest rate. This still leaves the question of what interest rate to use. The opportunity cost to the family which invests in education above the eighth grade might be considered to be the return which could alternatively have been earned by investing in common stocks. In 1959 this return was approximately 10 per cent for manufacturing companies after taxes.[5] The rate of return was a little higher in 1949 but probably was lower in 1939. For present purposes a discount rate of 10 per cent for all three years is highly convenient, and seems reasonably appropriate.

ESTIMATES OF HUMAN CAPITAL

Division of excess incomes attributable to education above the eighth grade by ten per cent gives the capital values shown in Table 8-2. Some comparisons of the present estimates with other estimated totals for the United States as a whole may be of interest.

4. Roy L. Lassiter, Jr., "Some Aspects of the Valuation of and Investment in Human Capital in the Southeastern United States 1939-1959," a paper presented in November, 1963, at the annual meeting of the Southern Economic Association.

5. Federal Trade Commission, *Profit Rates of Manufacturing Corporations, 1947-1962.*

TABLE 8-2. ESTIMATED VALUE OF HUMAN CAPITAL

Region and Group	Estimated Value ($ billion)		
	1939	1949	1959
South			
White males	18.6	48.3	129.0
White females	6.4	21.1	50.4
Non-white males	0.5	1.4	5.1
Non-white females	0.4	2.0	5.9
TOTAL	25.9	72.8	190.4
Non-South			
White males	61.0	127.6	305.2
White females	24.8	57.1	126.4
Non-white males	0.5	1.8	10.1
Non-white females	0.3	1.7	8.4
TOTAL	86.6	188.2	450.1
U.S. TOTAL	112.5	261.0	640.5

Weisbrod[6] obtained an estimated net value of $1,055 billion for males in 1950 when he used a 10 per cent discount rate. The capital value of males with income in 1949, as shown in Table 8-2 is only $179.1 billion. As already stated, a major reason for the large difference is that Weisbrod capitalizes all money earnings (in excess of consumption by the earner himself) whereas the present estimates are a capitalization only of excess earnings attributable to (or at least associated with) education beyond the eighth grade.

The general magnitude of the present estimates is more nearly in line with Professor T. W. Schultz's estimates of the "total value of the stock of education of the labor force."[7] These estimates, which are in 1956 prices, were made by valuing at cost an "equivalent school year" and multiplying the aggregate years of schooling in the labor force by this value. Schultz's estimates for 1940, 1950, and 1957 were $248 billion, $359 billion, and $535 billion, respectively. When the change in prices is considered, these figures seem

6. *Op. cit.*, p. 433.
7. "Education and Economic Growth," in *Social Forces Influencing American Education* (Chicago: University of Chicago Press, 1961), p. 73.

to be of the same order of magnitude as those in Table 8-2. However, the procedure employed by Schultz gives substantial weight (33 per cent in 1940) to elementary education. If an inference from these two sets of data is valid, it would be that the internal rate of return from investment in all education is well above 10 per cent, since value of schooling in terms of earnings capitalized at this rate would have been well above cost of the associated education if earnings attributable to the first eight years of schooling had not been omitted in the present study.[8] Since estimates in Table 8-2 were not prepared for this purpose, the results of more specific studies of the return to investment in education are likely to be more dependable.[9]

Like other comparisons of the relative rates of growth of material and human capital, the present study indicates a more rapid growth of the latter. National wealth (reproducible and non-reproducible, both private and public) has been estimated at $1682.9 billion in 1958, $900.2 billion in 1949, and $395.6 billion in 1939, in prices current in each of these years.[10] According to these figures, the stock of material wealth was 4.25 times as great in 1958 as in 1939. According to the present estimates of human capital values (also in current prices), the 1959 stock of immaterial capital was 5.69 times as large as the 1939 stock.

GROWTH OF HUMAN CAPITAL IN THE SOUTH

In earlier chapters it was tentatively concluded that the South is gaining in its share of human capital in spite of its declining share of all employed persons. This was inferred from the increase in the region's share of (white)

8. A brief discussion of cost and value on an investment project is contained in M. R. Colberg, D. R. Forbush, and G. R. Whitaker, *Business Economics: Principles and Cases* (Homewood, Ill.: Richard D. Irwin, 1964), p. 591.

9. Since completion of the present study, Gary S. Becker has published an excellent book, *Human Capital* (New York: Columbia University Press, 1964). He estimated the rate of return to an average college entrant to be of the order of 10 to 12 per cent per annum (p. 154).

10. *Statistical Abstract of the United States, 1963*, Table 465, p. 346, and *Historical Statistics of the United States, Colonial Times to 1957*, p. 151.

college graduates and the increase in the regional share of persons in professional and managerial occupations. This preliminary inference is confirmed by the data of Table 8-3 which show the proportion of the nation's stock of human capital resident in the South.

TABLE 8-3. VALUE OF HUMAN CAPITAL
SOUTH AS A PER CENT OF U.S. IN EACH CATEGORY

	Year		
Group	1939	1949	1959
White males	23	27	30
White females	21	27	29
Non-white males	50	44	34
Non-white females	57	54	41
TOTAL	23	28	30

Source: Calculated from Table 8-2.

Since more than 94 per cent of the region's immaterial capital is embodied in white residents, the sharp increases for whites caused the South's share of all human capital to increase substantially from 1939 to 1949 and more moderately from 1949 to 1959. World War II was undoubtedly a major factor in the former, while large-scale defense and space activities have certainly contributed to the more recent gain.

HUMAN CAPITAL OF NON-WHITE PERSONS

Table 8-3 shows a sharp decline in the South's share of immaterial capital embodied in both non-white men and non-white women. Most of this loss can be considered a capital export from the South, although measurement of migration according to educational status is difficult, as was pointed out in Chapter 4. However, it can be calculated from Table 8-2 that the South in 1959 had $4.8 billion less human capital embodied in non-whites than it would have had if the 1939 share of the nation's stock of this resource had merely been maintained. The region's export of capital, viewed this way, was somewhat greater for non-white males than for non-white females. An assessment of the general magnitude of this capital loss by the South can perhaps be made by comparing it with the $2.32 billion of new capital expenditures in manufacturing in the South in 1958 (Table II, Appendix). That is, the loss of non-white human capital in two decades was equivalent in value to about two years gross investment in all manufacturing in the South.

It was pointed out in Chapter 5 that about 60 per cent of all non-white professional, technical, and kindred workers in the South in 1959 were elementary and high school teachers. If the reduction in extent of school segregation in the South is associated with a sharp reduction in the employment of non-white school teachers—as it may well be— a further loss of investment in non-white teachers is in sight for the region. The loss may well be national and personal also unless the non-southern states are willing to hire displaced Negro teachers to a greater extent than has been the demonstrated practice.

HUMAN CAPITAL AND THE FEDERAL GOVERNMENT

The South's relative gain in total human capital seems quite certain to continue, especially in view of the ambitious space program. Florida, Texas, Louisiana, Mississippi, and Alabama will have more than 45,000 permanent employees at government sites in 1969, according to *U.S. News and World Report*.[11] A high percentage of these will be filled by university graduates. Multiplier effects in the immediate vicinity of the principal centers of space-related activity will provide many additional positions (of a less human capital intensive nature, however). Part of the region's ultimate gain from space exploration activities was, of course, already reflected in the 1960 census data which have been used.

Other federal government activities have great effects on both the total stock of human capital and its regional location. It is beyond the scope of the present study to assess

11. July 20, 1964, p. 65.

the effects of educational aid to veterans, placement of defense contracts, research and development grants and contracts, grants to graduate students, government employment, foreign aid, and many other important activities. It is clear, however, that some federal laws and practices are unfavorable to the movement of human capital into the South, or its retention by the region.

Federal minimum-wage legislation, insofar as it applies to manufacturing at least, has as its primary political motivation, neutralization of the force of the South's labor surplus in attracting plants at the expense of other regions. Adverse effects on employment are especially great in rural areas of the South, and federal minimum wage laws may thus contribute to the rural poverty which is currently receiving so much attention in political circles.[12] The loss of jobs in the South (and more importantly, the failure to secure an appropriate number of new jobs) resulting from federal minimum wage laws probably has relatively minor effects on human capital because the industries most affected employ relatively few professional persons. Employment impacts tend to be concentrated in such industries as textiles, apparel, leather products and furniture, where the contribution of professional persons is relatively small, as was shown in Table 6-5.

Federal minimum wage laws probably have a more unfavorable effect on well-educated non-whites in the South than on well-educated whites because the latter are not highly complementary to the types of capital equipment (e.g., textile machinery) which these laws tend to keep out of the South, while the former tend to be strongly complementary to the relatively unskilled persons who may be forced to leave the South. This is to say that Negro human capital tends to consist of investment in teachers, nurses, preachers and others who are affected strongly by employment opportunities of poorly-educated Negroes.

The Area Redevelopment program probably has also mainly an indirect effect on the location of human capital.

12. M. R. Colberg, "Minimum Wage Effects on Florida's Economic Development," *Journal of Law and Economics*, III (October, 1960), pp. 106-117.

Emphasis is on federal assistance which will provide substantial numbers of jobs for relatively unskilled persons rather than for well-educated persons. The South has a somewhat larger proportion of eligible counties than has the rest of the country.[13] Whether the effect on labor and human capital in the region will be favorable or unfavorable relative to the non-South depends on the actual administration of the law. It is interesting to note in this connection that the Small Business Administration also runs a distressed areas program in which firms in "areas of substantial unemployment" are eligible for loans at a lower interest rate than firms elsewhere. In general this discrimination in interest rates is unfavorable to southern economic development in that industrial "areas of substantial unemployment" are largely in the North and West. Low rural incomes in the South do not have a similar influence in securing preferential SBA rates.[14] To say the least, the various federal laws which affect regional economic development are frequently inconsistent and partially self-defeating.

13. M. R. Colberg, "Area Redevelopment and Related Progerms: Effects on the South," in *Essays in Southern Economic Development,* ed. by M. L. Greenhut and T. Whitman (Chapel Hill: University of North Carolina Press, 1964), p. 371.

14. *Ibid.,* p. 382.

Second thoughts, they say, are generally the best.
—Cicero, *Philippica*

CHAPTER IX
CONCLUSIONS

THIS STUDY has attempted to shed some further light on three matters of current interest: (1) southern economic development in recent years, (2) the value of human capital and its regional movement, and (3) some economic aspects of racial segregation and desegregation. Special attention has been paid to the teaching profession because of its great importance in the South in connection with the last matter. Relatively little emphasis has been placed on the problems of uneducated and impecunious persons, upon which other studies are known to be concentrating. Some theoretical implications of treating human capital as a separate factor of production, and a reconsideration of the concept of labor intensive industry, have also been included.

An attempt has been made to retain labor as a factor of production by assuming that the first eight years of schooling serve only to improve an individual's ability to be an effective and employable laborer or to provide the basis for subsequent schooling. Only post-elementary schooling is considered to build human capital. As a consequence, the earning power of a college graduate is considered to be only in part a return on his immaterial capital. His earning power above what it would presumably have been with only eight years of schooling is counted as a return on such capital. This follows the lead of Nassau Senior and other early economists who observed that the return to educated persons is a combination of wages and interest. The consequent division between labor and human capital is necessarily an arbitrary one which also contains the tacit assumption that an individual who graduates from high school or college would have had the same income, had he quit after elementary school, as an individual in the same sex, race, age, and regional category who actually did stop his education at that point. Probably the earning power of graduates of high schools and universities is inherently better than that of persons who stop their schooling in eight years or less. However, common observation also indicates that many well-educated persons would have been particularly ineffective as wage earners if they had not gone beyond the eighth grade.

Much of the work that has been done in the field of human capital is directed toward estimating the rate of return on investment in education, including elementary schooling. The present study has not concentrated on this problem, although it was noted in the previous chapter that this return would apparently be well above 10 per cent. Instead, human capital is conceived to be a resource which is considerably more mobile than either material capital or labor. As a result of its high mobility, human capital is unlikely to be either relatively abundant or scarce in any particular region within the United States but is likely instead to be well-allocated at all times. According to accepted theory, labor should be moving from the South to other parts of the country and material capital should be moving toward the South in order to take advantage of labor surpluses. As a further theoretical proposition it has been suggested here that human capital should be moving to the South if it is more complementary to material capital and out of the South if it is more complementary to labor.

Unfortunately, it is difficult to measure regional migration, according to educational status, from one census to the next, especially because many people also "migrate" from lower to higher educational groups. Also, available statistics do not clearly distinguish between all different levels of degrees granted, nor can one assume that students resident in a region acquire their higher education in the same region. It has been necessary in the main to measure changes in the South's share of the nation's college graduates, of professional and managerial personnel, and of calculated value of human capital in order to infer what movements have taken place. Such inter-regional changes are due in part to intra-regional activities, however, instead of actual movement. That is, a region can gain in its share of college graduates by educating its own residents to a greater extent than other regions are doing, as well as by being a net importer of persons with degrees.

Human capital embodied in white persons appears to be complementary in the main to the material capital which is moving southward. Human capital embodied in Negroes in the South has been more complementary to labor, due especially to the importance of segregated schooling during the period (1939-1959) to which most of the statistics used have pertained. These complementarities contributed to the substantial gains in the region's share of white human capital, shown in Table 8-3, and the declines in the share of non-white human capital shown in the same table.

EFFECTS OF DESEGREGATION IN EDUCATION

Quite apart from any considerations of the propriety of segregated education, there is no question but that this custom has been a major factor in causing non-white women to acquire college degrees in the South to a much greater extent than have non-white men. A further factor has been the poor opportunities open to Negro female high school graduates in the South. Many have continued to work as domestic servants, whereas secretarial and clerical opportunities, for example, are usually open to white girls in the South upon graduation from high school. Consequently, the excess earnings attributable to college degrees, especially for Negro women in the South, have been especially high and have provided a strong incentive to enter and to finish college. Permanent income prospects, and low foregone earnings while attending college, have been responsible for the surprisingly good showing of southern Negro women with respect to acquiring university degrees. Negro men have acquired much less education, and those who have secured higher degrees have not been complementary to manufacturing capital to a substantial extent.

There is danger that rapid desegregation of southern schools will be equivalent to the rapid dismantling of a protective tariff in its effects on a protected industry. It was estimated (Chapter 5) that about 37,000 teaching positions for non-whites were traceable in 1959 to the higher propensity of the South to hire non-white teachers because of segregation in education. (The amount of human capital associated with these positions is in the neighborhood of one billion dollars.) Large regional, national, and personal losses of immaterial capital will be incurred if the South adopts the demonstrated non-southern pattern of hiring teachers in legally unsegregated schools, and if, further, non-southern schools are unwilling to hire displaced Negro teachers. According to calculations made by the author from 1960 census data, South Dakota, Nebraska, Iowa, Connecticut, Wisconsin, and Massachusetts provided especially few opportunities for non-white teachers in relation to their non-white school-age populations. In part this is due to segregation of students on the basis of religion. Racial and religious segregation in schooling are apt to go hand in hand, inasmuch as few Negro students attend private schools. In larger part, the lack of teaching opportunities for non-whites is due to government discrimination which, so far as teaching goes, is greater outside the South. The important means of discrimination is not the rate of pay, but the number of teaching positions. Actually non-white female teachers even in the South have higher incomes than white female teachers, on the average, because of their greater urban concentration.

The South has been acquiring an increasing percentage of the nation's manufacturing activity. One measure of the increasing contribution of the region's material capital to manufacturing is found in the South's gain of annual quasi-rent (value added minus payroll) from 17.2 per cent of the national total in 1939 to 22.4 per cent in 1958. Most of the southern states shared in this improvement relative to the United States as a whole. However, the associated gain in manufacturing employment in the South was not sufficient to offset the loss in farm employment. An outmigration of labor (principally Negro) from the South and an inmigration of white human capital was the result of these and other economic forces in effect since 1939.

One often hears politicians (and even economists) say that a state or region should seek only "high wage industry" and should avoid "sweatshops." This is a dangerous fallacy which neglects the important concept of comparative advantage. Regions with large surpluses of ordinary labor require the types of industry that employ much ordinary labor at rates of pay which will be well below that of industries where skill requirements are high. That is, truly labor intensive rather than human capital intensive industry is needed by many communities.

According to Table 6-2, the ten industries in which the South's share of national value added by manufacture increased most between 1939 and 1958 were: textiles, tobacco products, petroleum products, rubber and plastic products, chemicals and allied products, paper and allied products, apparel, furniture and fixtures, electrical machinery, and transportation equipment. Of these, textiles, apparel, and furniture manufacturing appear to be the most labor intensive. Transportation equipment (except trailers), electrical machinery, and petroleum products make very substantial use of professionally trained persons whose services should be considered largely those of capital instead of labor. The tobacco industry uses relatively little of either labor or human capital at the manufacturing level (but is probably less highly mechanized at the earlier and later stages).

EXPORT INDUSTRIES

Calculations made in Chapter 6 of the contribution of professional persons to value added by manufacture help provide an answer to Leontief's paradox, i.e., that United States exports are labor intensive while our imports are capital intensive. Irving Kravis[1] listed chemicals, rubber, metals, machinery and instruments, printing and publishing, transportation equipment, and petroleum and coal products as "high wage industries" from which United States exports have been consistently drawn. These industries all utilize professionally trained persons to a much greater extent than do the manufacturers of tobacco products, textiles, apparel, leather products, furniture. The same is true of some other "truly labor intensive" manufactures. When the contributions of material and human capital are added, it appears that all or most of the principal export industries listed by Kravis have more than half of their value added by capital. In general, when a new look is taken at the factors of production in order to separate the contribution of labor and human capital, the United States appears to be an exporter of capital intensive goods. The writer does not wish to imply, however, that estimates made in the present study are sufficient for a full appraisal of the Leontief paradox.

GOVERNMENT INTERVENTION

Federal minimum-wage legislation has been supported mainly by labor unions, northern and western Congressmen, and business interests in these regions, in order to reduce competition from southern labor-surplus areas.

1. "Wages and Foreign Trade," *Review of Economics and Statistics,* XXXVIII, February, 1956, pp. 26-27.

The unemployment problem among displaced farm workers, especially Negroes, has been made more severe by this interference with the price system. However, northern cities themselves are bearing much of the ultimate burden of unemployment among poorly-educated migrants from the South. The Area Redevelopment program can in part be considered an attempt to make it unnecessary for displaced farm workers and others to migrate in an attempt to secure jobs. However, political compromises have caused such a large part of the country to be designated as distressed that the program has little prospect of much success. Also, the "anti-pirating" provisions are designed to prevent federal aid even for the movement of a plant from a prosperous area to a truly depressed area. This provision was aimed mainly against the South. Similarly, provisions of the Small Business Administration Act are somewhat unfavorable to the South so far as the preferential interest rate goes.

Although several federal laws are relatively unfavorable to the employment of ordinary labor in the South, federal activity in the field of space exploration is highly favorable to well-trained people in the region. Also, expanding government employment—which tends to be human capital intensive—in Washington, D.C., itself has been favorable to adjoining southern states.

The new emphasis on the general idea of combatting poverty is more appropriate than that of aiding particular industries (agriculture) or regions (Area Redevelopment). When aid is not given on a personal basis much of it is certain to go to those who do not need it. (Large federal payments to wealthy farmers are a prime example.) However, a federally sponsored anti-poverty program would hold more promise if it were not accompanied by countervailing efforts to raise the federal minimum wage, to maintain high agricultural prices, to restore "fair trading," to encourage unionization of labor, and to minimize the power of local governmental units which are best able to determine who are actually the poor.

APPENDIX

TABLE I.   SOUTHERN AND NATIONAL MANUFACTURING QUASI-
RENTS ($ BILLION)

Region and Year	Value Added	Total Payroll	Quasi-Rent
1939: South Atlantic	2.22	1.07	1.15
East South Central	0.82	0.39	0.43
West South Central	0.82	0.36	0.46
United States	24.49	12.70	11.79
1947: South Atlantic	6.94	3.37	3.57
East South Central	2.88	1.36	1.52
West South Central	3.03	1.33	1.70
United States	74.29	39.70	34.59
1954: South Atlantic	10.66	5.48	5.18
East South Central	4.70	2.29	2.41
West South Central	5.72	2.68	3.04
United States	117.03	62.96	54.07
1958: South Atlantic	14.29	6.94	7.35
East South Central	6.40	2.99	3.41
West South Central	7.79	3.48	4.31
United States	141.27	73.74	67.53

Source: U.S. Bureau of the Census, 1958 *Census of Manufactures,* vol. III,
Area Statistics.

TABLE II.   SOUTHERN AND NATIONAL NEW CAPITAL EXPENDITURES
IN MANUFACTURING ($ BILLION)

Region	1947	1954	1958
South Atlantic	0.68	0.79	0.99
East South Central	0.26	0.40	0.47
West South Central	0.46	0.72	0.86
South Total	1.40	1.91	2.32
United States Total	6.00	7.81	9.08

Source: U.S. Bureau of the Census, *1958 Census of Manufactures*, vol. III,
Area Statistics.

TABLE III.   MANUFACTURING QUASI-RENTS IN SOUTHERN STATES
($ MILLION)

State	1939			1958		
	Value Added	Payroll	Quasi-Rent	Value Added	Payroll	Quasi-Rent
Alabama	245.58	114.71	130.87	1770.51	887.20	883.31
Arkansas	66.44	33.35	33.09	591.75	288.15	303.60
Delaware	54.08	29.11	24.97	419.83	191.78	228.05
D.C.	43.37	24.92	18.45	198.09	109.65	88.44
Florida	115.89	55.36	60.53	1410.84	656.60	754.24
Georgia	280.03	142.02	138.01	2102.33	1062.50	1039.83
Kentucky	186.48	89.00	97.48	1781.97	693.17	1088.80
Louisiana	198.52	85.27	113.25	1429.58	618.09	811.49
Maryland	420.59	209.19	211.40	2379.41	1241.82	1137.59
Mississippi	72.66	36.50	36.16	642.18	353.02	289.16
North Carolina	544.18	245.88	298.30	3083.45	1445.57	1637.88
Oklahoma	101.78	47.17	54.61	725.00	367.94	357.06
South Carolina	169.29	103.17	66.12	1360.14	726.64	633.50
Tennessee	318.38	149.53	168.85	2207.07	1058.36	1148.71
Texas	448.52	196.74	251.78	5045.16	2208.17	2836.99
Virginia	376.26	150.36	225.90	2122.65	948.96	1173.69
West Virginia	213.28	113.66	99.62	1214.78	560.14	654.64

Source: U.S. Bureau of the Census, *1958 Census of Manufactures,* vol. III, *Area
Statistics.*

TABLE IV. DEGREES EARNED BY WHITES AND NON-WHITES IN THE SOUTH
1950-51 THROUGH 1957-58

State	Academic Year	White		Non-White	
		Male	Female	Male	Female
Alabama	1950-51	3942	1725	430	559
	51-52	2862	1672	467	851
	52-53	2416	1598	356	1067
	53-54	2368	1460	356	1111
	54-55	2361	1402	380	952
	55-56	2689	1497	402	922
	56-57	3363	1596	494	731
	57-58	3401	1629	429	645
Arkansas	1950-51	2098	930	132	194
	51-52	1628	1097	98	192
	52-53	1482	997	92	214
	53-54	1306	926	120	251
	54-55	1342	940	101	217
	55-56	1515	920	116	183
	56-57	1645	912	126	156
	57-58	1981	951	132	185
Florida	1950-51	4838	1561	277	452
	51-52	3622	1569	174	323
	52-53	3260	1400	167	361
	53-54	3063	1406	153	338
	54-55	2732	1329	193	399
	55-56	3106	1441	202	409
	56-57	3784	1834	237	326
	57-58	4129	1654	234	358
Georgia	1950-51	4407	1372	433	506
	51-52	3567	1550	329	647
	52-53	3353	1783	302	639
	53-54	2881	1606	245	803
	54-55	2735	1469	242	822
	55-56	2823	1433	287	643
	56-57	3319	1555	349	650
	57-58	3594	1640	327	572
Kentucky	1950-51	3637	1315	62	57
	51-52	2971	1252	47	45
	52-53	2513	1309	34	49
	53-54	2377	1499	27	41
	54-55	2444	1378	32	61

127

TABLE IV (Cont.)

State	Academic Year	White		Non-White	
		Male	Female	Male	Female
	55-56	2637	1641	54	48
	56-57	3081	1862	35	49
	57-58	3449	2035	43	38
Louisiana	1950-51	3828	1463	387	364
	51-52	2882	1395	292	453
	52-53	2439	1066	274	362
	53-54	2455	1480	278	761
	54-55	2721	1475	334	832
	55-56	2908	1573	400	986
	56-57	3205	1678	449	807
	57-58	3462	1672	381	746
Mississippi	1950-51	2247	1050	197	183
	51-52	1691	1012	169	240
	52-53	1380	1013	142	239
	53-54	1410	1000	123	435
	54-55	1471	1054	165	379
	55-56	1718	1003	191	483
	56-57	1960	1024	256	574
	57-58	2078	1098	289	638
North Carolina	1950-51	4495	2114	669	851
	51-52	3827	1993	558	871
	52-53	3336	2172	499	873
	53-54	3485	2265	430	987
	54-55	3195	2105	428	948
	55-56	3622	2276	481	883
	56-57	4224	2430	505	989
	57-58	4817	2476	574	877
Oklahoma	1950-51	5506	1935	69	84
	51-52	3904	1883	57	66
	52-53	3473	1834	58	48
	53-54	3336	1696	42	53
	54-55	3284	1659	31	50
	55-56	3827	1738	47	45
	56-57	4325	1760	38	41
	57-58	4626	1826	41	31
South Carolina	1950-51	2686	1196	285	550
	51-52	1976	661	220	416

TABLE IV (CONT.)

State	Academic Year	White		Non-White	
		Male	Female	Male	Female
	52-53	1839	796	206	603
	53-54	1842	919	201	614
	54-55	1983	899	176	589
	55-56	2092	984	250	751
	56-57	2258	990	270	644
	57-58	2343	1010	289	557
Tennessee	1950-51	4550	1733	463	411
	51-52	3549	1846	334	500
	52-53	3093	1881	301	459
	53-54	3135	1956	274	464
	54-55	3128	1925	312	498
	55-56	3506	3062	343	430
	56-57	3887	2236	383	409
	57-58	4261	2342	406	456
Texas	1950-51	13316	5247	563	862
	51-52	10452	5250	394	789
	52-53	9328	4927	461	778
	53-54	9231	4574	446	820
	54-55	9270	4700	432	768
	55-56	10293	5021	447	756
	56-57	11641	5249	417	582
	57-58	12703	5526	476	616
Virginia	1950-51	4052	1715	422	481
	51-52	3102	1735	318	576
	52-53	2785	1673	295	454
	53-54	2508	1573	261	476
	54-55	2560	1607	277	370
	55-56	2701	1667	266	432
	56-57	3033	1794	261	401
	57-58	3406	2024	286	383
West Virginia	1950-51	2491	1137	218	228
	51-52	1832	1014	147	169
	52-53	1540	1012	126	167
	53-54	1337	1021	125	137
	54-55	1346	983	112	129
	55-56	1582	974	102	111
	56-57	1731	1131	118	85
	57-58	1952	1203	107	75

TABLE IV (CONT.)

State	Academic Year	White		Non-White	
		Male	Female	Male	Female
South	1950-51	62093	24493	4607	5782
	51-52	47865	23929	3604	6138
	52-53	42237	23461	3313	6313
	53-54	40734	23381	3081	7291
	54-55	40572	22925	3215	7014
	55-56	45019	25230	3588	7082
	56-57	51456	26051	3927	6444
	57-58	56202	27086	4014	6177
TOTAL		386,178	196,556	29,349	52,241

Source: *Earned Degrees Conferred* (Washington: U.S. Office of Education, Annually, 1950-51 through 1957-58). Data show bachelor's and first professional degree, combined. Computed by author on the basis of lists of white and non-white colleges and universities in the South. These figures are subject to some error in racial breakdown due to incomplete segregation.

TABLE V. SAMPLE COMPUTATION OF PER CENT OF VALUE ADDED BY LABORERS, PROFESSIONALS, AND MATERIAL CAPITAL (EXAMPLE: NORTH CAROLINA—APPAREL AND RELATED PRODUCTS)

I. Percent of Value Added by Material Capital

Value Added by Manufacture (1958)[1]	$155,244,000
Total Payroll (1958)[1]	69,742,000
Value Added by Material Capital	$ 45,502,000

Percent of Value Added by Material Capital: 39.5%

II. Per Cent of Value Added by Laborers and Professionals

A. ESTIMATED TOTAL PAYROLL, 1959

Number Employed[2]		Median Earnings in Apparel Industry[3]		Estimated Payroll (Median Considered Mean)	
Males	Females	Males	Females	Males	Females
5,393	27,617	$2,974	$1,953	$15,068,042	$53,936,001

B. PROFESSIONAL PERSONS EMPLOYED, 1959

Job Classification	Number		Median Earnings[4]		Estimated Total Earnings	
	Males	Females	Males	Females	Males	Females
Accountants	28	16	$5,939	$3,597	$ 166,292	$ 57,552
Draftsmen	4	16	4,944	2,567	19,776	41,072
Engineers	47	—	7,364	—	346,108	—
Other Technicians	4	4	7,341	—	29,364	11,164
Personnel Workers	8	—	5,801	—	46,408	—
Other Professional	4	40	4,587	3,149	18,348	125,960
Salaried Managers	355	58	7,934	2,667	2,816,570	154,686
TOTAL					$3,442,866	$390,434

C. Total Professional Payroll, 1959: $3,833,300

Professional Payroll as Per Cent of Total Payroll, 1959: 5.56%

Estimated 1958 Professional Payroll (5.56% of $69,742,000): $3,877,655

$3,877,655 ÷ $115,244,000 = 3.4% of Value Added by Professionals

100% — 3.4% — 39.5% = 57.1% of Value Added by Labor

1. Source: *1958 Census of Manufactures*, vol. III.

2. *U.S. Census of Population*, 1960; *Detailed Characteristics, North Carolina*, Table 125.

3. *Ibid.*, Table 130.

4. *Ibid.*, Table 124 (pertains to entire profession in North Carolina).

TABLE VI
1939

Income Category	Number with 12 Years of Schooling and with Income	Total Excess Income of Group ($ million)	Number with 16 or more years of Schooling and with Income	Total Excess Income of Group ($ million)
WHITE MALES				
South	1,050,240	510.5	413,240	531.0
Non-South	4,364,980	1714.1	1,399,560	1703.9
WHITE FEMALES				
South	873,080	240.2	253,220	137.0
Non-South	3,407,880	876.8	691,380	583.7
NON-WHITE MALES				
South	68,140	7.7	23,100	11.9
Non-South	75,080	11.5	15,740	8.1
NON-WHITE FEMALES				
South	81,540	5.8	26,120	12.3
Non-South	72,930	5.2	11,740	8.2

Note: The number of persons shown in this table is far below the total number with income, since only those with precisely twelve and sixteen or more years of formal education are included here.

1949

Income Category	Number with 12 Years of Schooling and other Income	Total Excess Income of Group ($ million)	Number with 16 or more years of Schooling and with Income	Total Excess Income of Group ($ million)
WHITE MALES				
South	1,612,090	1352.5	626,550	1352.2
Non-South	6,489,750	3577.1	2,031,600	3566.1
WHITE FEMALES				
South	1,131,520	765.2	344,690	480.4
Non-South	4,756,800	2214.2	947,480	1156.2
NON-WHITE MALES				
South	111,000	26.6	35,520	32.5
Non-South	207,730	53.8	36,270	24.8
NON-WHITE FEMALES				
South	110,880	22.5	50,160	74.8
Non-South	200,100	48.3	29,220	32.3

1959

Income Category	Number with 12 Years of Schooling and with Income	Total Excess Income of Group ($ million)	Number with 16 or more years of Schooling and with Income	Total Excess Income of Group ($ million)
WHITE MALES				
South	2,526,769	3,319.0	1,106,529	4,164.1
Non-South	8,030,587	6,734.0	3,065,347	10,965.2
WHITE FEMALES				
South	1,851,534	1,869.8	522,237	1,206.1
Non-South	5,770,439	4,616.5	1,409,550	3,096.8
NON-WHITE MALES				
South	241,878	111.8	59,189	123.8
Non-South	438,697	291.3	96,689	171.3
NON-WHITE FEMALES				
South	238,903	71.0	94,218	259.5
Non-South	398,301	291.1	70,074	178.9

INDEX

A

Abstinence, as conduct, 25; and human capital, 25; painfulness, 25; Socialist criticism, 25

Agriculture, employment decline, 11; capital movement toward South, 37

Aircraft industry, use of professionals, 86

Apparel, gain in Southeast, 74; plants in Florida, 75; regional moves, 75

Area Redevelopment Act, and human capital, 116; and need for migration, 124

Areas, problems in defining, 5n

Aristotle, 42

Arkansas, relatively low per capita income in, 9

B

Bachelors' degrees, not separately reported, 45

Becker, G., 24, 31, 70

Birth rate, non-white, 13

C

Cannan, E., 22

Capital, as wage fund, 21; definition of, 26; mineral industries, 38; positions complementary to, 54. *See also* Human capital

Capital expenditures, South's share, tab. 3-2, 35; Southern and national, App. tab. II, 126

Capital goods, mobility of, 27n

Capital intensive activities, 30, 75

Cash flow, defined, 34; future in South, 36

Chemical industry, largest in South, 78

Chicago metropolitan area, share in capital expenditures, 36n

Chicago School, and *ad hoc* definitions, 5, 6n

Cicero, 118

Classical economists, use of term profits, 21

Classification, *ad hoc*, 23-24

Clergymen, Negro, 53

College education, and earnings of Negro women, 99

College graduates, embody human capital, 42; inventory of in South and U.S., tab. 4-2, 50; employment of, 51; South's share, 51

Common stocks, return on, 111

Comparative advantage, and wage rates, 122

Complementarity, teachers and students, 56

D

Degrees, female white, 46; male white, 46; female non-white, 48;